JAHTIGUI
The Life and Music of Ali Farka Toure

COREY HARRIS

⋯ *Table of Contents* ⋯

A Brief History of Mali

The history of the region now known as Mali reaches back to the ancient Ghana empire, founded in the 4th century ACE. Encompassing what is now eastern Senegal, southwest Mali, and southern Mauritania, Ghana reached its zenith in the 10th century. The abundant trade in salt and gold that it conducted with Arab states across the Sahara made it fabulously wealthy. The Ghana empire fell apart by the 13th century. It was replaced by the Mali empire under the rule of the legendary Sundiata Keita, who united several disparate Mande kingdoms under one Impe rial throne. At this time, Mali comprised parts of what is now Guinea, Gambia, Sierra Leone, Liberia, Burkina Faso, Senegal, Mauritania, and the Ivory Coast. It is said that the name Mali comes from the many hippopotamuses that make the Joliba (Niger) river their home. The name may also come from the Malinke people, a Mande group closely related to the Bambara, the rulers of ancient and modern Mali.

The height of the Mali empire came in the 14th century under the great Mansa Musa (r. 1312-1337), whose pilgrimage to Mecca made Mali known far and wide. Stopping in Egypt with his vast caravan on his way to Mecca, he dropped so much gold on the local market that it was destabilized for years afterwards. Ancient Mali owed its riches to trade in gold and salt, two commodities which it had in abundance. Mansa Musa also captured Timbuktu from its nomadic Tuareg rulers, transforming it into a renowned center of Muslim scholarship. Islam had by now become the religion of trade with rulers finding it politically and economically expedient to profess the new, imported faith. Along with the renowned trading city of Djenne, Timbuktu had long played a vital role in the trans-Sahara trade. However, by the 17th century, the empire had disintegrated and the Tuareg re-established their domination of the former empire's northern reaches.

The Songhai empire began along the banks of the Niger river in northern Mali. Previously a vassal state of the powerful Gao empire that was founded in the ninth century, it reached its peak under Sonni Ali Ber (r. 1464-1492), who captured Timbuktu again from the Tuareg. Succeeding Sonni Ali was Askia ("the usurper") Muhammed I (r. 1492-1528). Subsequent rulers were not as effective and the empire began a slow decline. Soon Morocco set its sights on the great wealth of the region, and in 1591 Songhai fell to invading armies who made the long march across the desert from the Moroccan capital in Fez. Gao, Timbuktu, and Djenne all fell to the Moroccans, who killed or exiled the intellectual elite of Timbuktu, thus ending the legendary city's status as a center of Islamic learning.

The Arma, a mix of conscripted soldiers of Moroccan, Scottish, Irish, and Moorish origin emerged as a military caste which controlled the rural areas for the occupying Moroccan forces based in the capital city of Fez (Ali Farka Toure was a direct descendant of the Arma.) The Arma were converts to Islam; eventually they intermarried with the local population and adopted Songhai language and customs. Ultimately, they were abandoned by their Morrocan superiors who returned to Fez. The local population absorbed the Arma, who nevertheless retained traces of their origins in the distinct tongue known as Zarma. By the 18th century, the Songhai empire had collapsed into separate petty states.

The 19th century bore witness to the reign of the Tucoulor, who under the zealous al-Haj Umar Tall waged a holy war to bring the remaining non-Islamic populations of the region under the yoke of Islam. In 1862, his forces conquered Segou and Macina; the following year Timbuktu fell, its riches and intellectual traditions plundered. Al-Haj Umar died in 1864. By 1880 the French had began their domination of western Sudan, what would later become the Republic of Mali. Their chief adversary was the great Malinke (Mande) leader Samory Toure (grandfather of Guinean President Sekou Toure), who confounded French ambitions in the region from 1882-1898. With his ultimate capture and exile to the Congo, the French solidified their subjugation of the area's populations. The fall of Sikasso in 1898 finished the French conquest and turned a new page in the history of Mali.

Introduction

"Live for yourself and you will live in vain; live for others and you will live again."

- Bob Marley

Richmond, VA January, 2013

From the first time that I met Ali Farka Toure, I knew that I would never be the same again. He was already an icon of African music but there was something familiar in the way that he related to everyone and in the way he expressed his love of music and African culture. It was like meeting a long lost relative. We spent several hot days and nights in northern Mali singing and playing guitar, we broke bread together and we laughed together. Of course, his music made a huge impression upon me, but his outlook on life and his influence on the world around him proved to have the most lasting impact. His music was an expression of his life, a chronicle of his experiences. His music is more than entertainment. Ali's music is a force for education, promoting Malian unity as well as cultural and historical pride. Today's Mali faces an uncertain future

i

and ethnic tensions are on the rise. The lessons exemplified in Ali's life and music are no less potent than when he walked the earth.

The first time we crossed paths was in April 1994 at the New Orleans Jazz and Heritage Festival. I was a young street musician playing a short set at a stage inside a small tent for local artists. It was my first big break. A year earlier I had quit my job as a school teacher in rural Assumption Parish, LA and moved to New Orleans to try and make it in music. I got a job at Tower Records in the French Quarter and immersed myself in the music of the city and the world beyond, spending the greater part of my small monthly paycheck buying music to learn from. I had already heard his 1990 album, African Blues, and was immediately taken by how he played the guitar. It didn't sound like a guitar when he played it, but like some ancient stringed instrument from another world. I remember looking several times at the photo on the album cover, trying to figure out what was different about his guitar from the one that I played. My eyes couldn't believe what my ears were telling me. The same year that I performed at the Jazz Fest, Ali appeared with American guitarist Ry Cooder on *Talking Timbuktu* which was later awarded a Grammy. For many American audiences, unfamiliar with Ali Farka's music, Ry Cooder was the main attraction. I overheard a young college student say that he was going to hear Ry Cooder play with 'some African guy.' But for me, Ali Farka Toure was the undisputed star of the show. I was there to hear this African bluesman whose playing was unlike any music I had ever heard.

To hear his music, his singing and playing, the rhythms and chants was like hearing the mother tongue of all music. I was hearing a language that was embedded in my DNA, hovering at the edges of memory. Though he played the guitar, his skill on the fretboard transformed the instrument into something much older and ancient. The weeping strains of the ngoni, the clap of the calabash, and the heartbeat of the conga, the shouts and handclaps of the chorus -- it was all there, woven into his intricate guitar lines and heart-wrenching vocals. It seemed everyone was talking about this amazing guitarist and vocalist, 'the African John Lee Hooker.' Many even said that Ali learned how to play by listening to the music of this blues icon. Even though he was passionate about Black American music and John Lee Hooker in particular, this could not have been further from the truth.

After his performance he participated in a question and answer session where he was bombarded with questions from the largely white American audience about his view of the blues. Imagine the surprise when Ali stated plainly, "To me the blues is just a color. My music is older than the blues." As he surveyed the audience, his look was dead-pan and his words were a dry statement of fact. I was reminded of historian John Henrik Clarke when he said, "I only debate my equals. All others I teach." With two sentences he dismantled the western idea of what is the blues. He was telling them that the blues is not as old as they might think. It comes from a source that is much more ancient than most westerners can understand. Many listeners knew absolutely nothing of the debt that the blues owed to the music and culture of Africa and specifically Mali. Some were even hostile to the idea that this quintessentially American art form was not born in

America. Though Ali stated a simple fact, it was a provoca-
tive statement.In 2000 my first invitation to play in Mali
came from Boubacar Traore, the celebrated guitarist and
vocalist from Kayes, a town near the Senegalese border. A
year later I found myself back in Mali, this time with a film
crew employed by Martin Scorcese for the PBS series, The
Blues. This was my first trip to Niafunke, Ali's hometown
in the deserts outside of Timbuktu. We sat under a tree
on his farm on the banks of the Joliba (Niger) and played
and talked about history, music, culture, Mali and what it
means to be Black in America. His grasp of history was as-
tounding, measured not in terms of years, but millennia. I
was so taken by this experience that I talked with Ali about
returning the following year to collaborate on a record. He
supported me every step of the way, giving selflessly of his
time and welcoming me into his home with genuine Songhai hospitality.

In March of 2002 we recorded Mississippi to Mali, an
album that documented the meeting of the blues and the
music of northern Mali, Ali's music. Around this time Ali
told me that his days of traveling overseas to perform were
over. His immediate focus became the development of his
community. He continued to perform and record, though
less frequently. The last time I saw him was in 2004 in
France. Only fifteen months later he would die from the
bone cancer he had been fighting for several years. Many
people did not even know he was sick.Ever since he depart-
ed this life, my mind keeps going back to our session under
the tree during my first visit to Niafunke. That afternoon
he told me, "What I wish is that as you have come in peace
and prosperity, that you return in peace and prosperity to
make a difference to those around you so that they can see
the path. The path of peace and prosperity grounded in

reality and mutual agreement. And here (he points to the earth we are sitting on) are the roots." Since Ali spoke these words, I have given a lot of serious thought as to how I might best honor his wish. His craft, his works and his life were inseparable from the man that he was. He played not for the accolades, recognition nor financial gain but for the love of music and culture itself. He played to make a difference in the world. Behind this sublime musical mind lay a sincere belief in the power of music to educate, uplift and inform. This book is a small step towards the realization of the task that he set before me more than ten years ago as we sat in the shade next to the ancient river.

At the time of this writing, it is the beginning of 2013. Mali is a nation at war with its northern half. The weak government in Bamako has welcomed nearly two thousand French troops and thousands more from neighboring nations who will come to fight alongside them. France, the US and Mali's neighbors are intent on the 'restoration of the territorial integrity' of the modern Republic, though the US is wary of committing a large contingent of soldiers after its decade-long adventures Iraq and Afghanistan. The army of this former poster-child for African democracy is underpaid, underfunded and underequipped. The Islamist rebels rout them easily whenever they cross their path. A few days prior to this writing, French forces bombed the Islamic Police building in Ali's hometown of Niafunke in a bid to oust Islamist rebels who have taken over half of the country, an area larger than the size of Texas. I wonder what Ali would say. He worked the land with devotion; he played deeply spiritual music with passionate abandon. Now his land is occupied by Islamist militants with purported ties to Al-Qaeda, sharia law is enforced and all music is outlawed. Singers have been threatened with having their tongues cut out, and musical instruments are routinely destroyed. How the times do change. Nobody knows what the future holds for Mali, but war is certain. Mali's economy, heavily dependent on tourism, is all but ruined. Where there is no peace there can be no prosperity. Ali Farka Toure walked a righteous path and he made a difference in the lives of every one around him. If he were alive today, he would be a force for good amid the chaos and destruction. He loved all of Mali and would fight for unity and mutual understanding. It would pain him to see the ethnic divisions and the violence after so many years of peace. I pray that this book is a worthwhile addition to the understanding of one of Africa's most accomplished musicians and the ancient source of the blues.

DEFENDERS OF
THE FAITH

"Truth is the first victim of war."

- anonymous

$\mathcal{T}$he Tuareg are a nomadic Berber people (ima-
zighen "the free (or noble) people"; they call themselves
the kel-tamasheck. The speakers of tamasheck, (the Tuareg language) who are scattered across the Sahara and
the Sahel of Mali, Mauritania, Burkina Faso, Niger, Lybia
and Algeria. They are also known as 'the blue people' because of the indigo dye which colors their fabric and rubs
off on the skin. They are among the original inhabitants
of the region. When Arab armies invaded North Africa
the Tuareg were already there. Since the beginning of the
twentieth century, Malian Tuareg militants have rebelled
against those who sought to rule them and their vast desert homeland in the north. Some would call the vast ocean
of dunes in the north a wasteland but to the Tuareg it is
beloved as the 'Azawad', which refers to the vast desert
regions of Gao, Kidal, Timbuktu and a part of the region of
Mopti. The modern Republic of Mali has always been ruled
from the capitol of Bamako in southern Mali by the Bambara. Tuareg have long complained of the lack of effective
economic development programs and government neglect.

1

The first Tuareg rebellions began in the late nineteenth century against French colonial incursions into Tuareg lands. The Tuareg were eventually forced to sign treaties with the French in Mali (1905) and Niger (1917). Subsequent rebellions erupted in 1960 and in 1990, which were ended by treaties between Tuareg rebels and the governments of Mali and Niger.

Libyan leader Muammar Gadaffi was a generous patron of the Tuareg. He received several hundred fighters to serve in a special all-Tuareg battalion within the Libyan army. Indeed it was with Tuareg assistance that the Colonel and his family were able to survive for so long after being forced from power. When Gadaffi met his brutal end at the hands of Libyan rebels, anyone suspected of benefitting from or having worked for the old regime was in danger of being imprisoned or killed by militants of the new regime. This included not only the Tuareg soldiers and their families, but black and brown skinned Africans from many different nations. Among these were thousands of Black migrant workers who had no affiliation to Gadaffi whatsoever. Some Tuareg had fought for the National Transitional Council, while others had remained faithful to the old regime. When their Libyan sojourn had come to an end, they returned to Mali armed to the teeth with heavy machine guns, mortars and automatic weapons, ready to liberate the Azawad by force. This is exactly what several governments had feared: a massive influx of well-trained Tuareg fighters whose return threatened to destabilize the entire region and re-ignite old conflicts. In fact, Gadaffi's sponsorship relieved the Malian government of a major security problem, effectively removing a hostile force outside of the nation's borders. Though his patronage of the Tuareg lasted for several years, it was only a

2

temporary solution to the serious problem of instability in the north. The newly repatriated Tuareg rebel army joined with other anti-government elements, most notably the National Movement for Azawad (MNA) a political organization in existence prior to the most recent insurgency. They soon adopted a new name, the National Movement for the Liberation of the Azawad (MNLA). This new group was a combination of Tuareg nationalists, political activists and experienced soldiers. Though their backers were never publicly identified, the MNLA did not do this without the help of a hidden hand. Suspiciously, reporters covering the events were directed to an MNLA spokesman who conducted interviews over a satellite phone from an office in Paris. Many suspected a heavy French influence in the entire Malian debacle, and with good reason. France (and other Western powers) regularly waged proxy conflicts in their former colonies, reaping economic benefits from the resulting chaos. War is profitable.

At the same time a Tuareg Islamist group known as Ansar Dine (Defenders of the Faith) threw in their lot with the secular MNLA, coordinating their anti-government actions with the much larger group. Many observers have asserted that rich sheiks from the Persian Gulf nation of Qatar provide much of their financing. Ansar Dine was started by veteran Tuareg commander Iyad Ag Ghaly, who led the Popular Movement for the Liberation of Azawad (MPLA) in a rebellion that lasted from 1990 until he signed a formal truce with the Malian government in 1996. He is the cousin of AQIM commander Hamada Ag Hama. International media have made much of the presence of AQIM (Al Qaeda in the Islamic Maghreb), a group with roots in the decades-long Algerian conflict that has operated with near impunity in the vast deserts of northern Mali. They profit

3

handsomely from the heavy traffic in drugs and weaponry that moves through the desert on its way north. They and their allies in the north have made news and money with their high-profile abductions where captives are held for ransoms of several million dollars. There have also been killings of western captives. From the beginning, the two groups had different objectives. While the MNLA seeks independence or autonomy from the Republic of Mali, Ansar Dine's main objective is the imposition of Sharia law throughout all of Mali. There would later be intense disputes among both groups for supremacy, with the MNLA later declaring Ag Ghaly a criminal whose "theocratic regime" was against the "foundations of Tuareg culture and civilization."

There has also been much commentary on the differences between individual Tuareg – referred to as 'lighter skinned' by the color-obsessed Western media – and other Malian ethnic groups such as the Bambara. In truth, the Tuareg are not a monolithic group. Like any African population with a long history of migration -- African-Americans come to mind -- the Tuareg display a wide variety of skin tones, from olive, to brown to jet black. The darker-skinned Tuareg are often referred to as *bella*, a Songhai word meaning slave. This is partly due to the long-abandoned practice of raiding neighboring communities and absorbing them into Tuareg society as slaves. Though modern-day divisions among the Tuareg do not strictly adhere to differences in skin color, concepts of class and status persist. There are twenty-one different Tuareg groups, and though the MNLA claims to fight for the Tuareg as a whole, many do not support them because of the chaos which ensued in the aftermath of the successful rebellion. Many peoples' property was seized or destroyed, their crops

4

and livelihoods were ruined. Indeed, of the many hundreds of thousands of refugees who fled to neighboring countries such as Niger, Maurtiania and Burkina Faso, the majority are Tuareg. But the land is not theirs alone. The conflict has also displaced thousands of Songhai, Peul, Bambara, Malian Arabs and others who also claim the north as their homeland. It is also reported that nearly a thousand Tuareg troops from the Malian army sought refuge in Niger, refusing to fight with the MNLA. Immediately after their repatriation, the Malian government sought to open a dialogue with the returned warriors. However it soon became clear that any negotiations with the Tuaregs would not be easy. After a long history of rebellion against the French and later the Mali Republic, they were intent on separation. The MNLA was clear in their position that the government of Mali must either allow the Azawad peoples their self-determination or they would take it themselves. In fact, the government's hold on the vast deserts of the north had always been tenuous, dependent upon several remote garrisons. When the Tuareg rebellion began to gather real strength in early 2012, it was these garrisons which were easily overran. The Tuaregs' strategy was to draw the soldiers into a confrontation in a remote outpost and then move to fill in the vacuum created when soldiers from other garrisons left to reinforce their comrades. Policing the vast emptiness of the Sahara desert was difficult for the government, where ancient trade routes are the lifelines for both legitimate and illicit commerce.

These Tuareg warriors were battle-hardened and naturally adapted to living and fighting in the desert. This was their tactical advantage. They began a game of cat and mouse with the army, attacking and occupying smaller towns (Menaka, Tessalit, Anderamboukane, Lere, and Ali

Farka Toure's hometown of Niafunke), retreating, regrouping and re-attacking in other areas. The army, already stretched thin in the north, could not be everywhere at once. Although the army had cooperated closely with the US military over the previous ten years, this training was useless against the chaos that was quickly consuming this ancient land. To make matters worse, many soldiers in the army were underpaid or not paid at all. Many others were sent to the front without adequate food or weaponry. Morale was extremely low among the troops. Media reported that large numbers of Tuaregs who had previously served in the Malian army switched sides. Many other soldiers simply deserted. It was against this backdrop that a large group of soldiers' wives in Bamako protested publicly about the conditions their husbands were forced to endure while fighting on the front lines. There were reports that the Malian president, Amadou Toumani Toure, was in the process of negotiating with the MNLA. Many soldiers saw his administration as the source of their problems. They thought that negotiation with the rebels was a sign of weakness. For the proud Bambara, the territorial integrity of Mali could never be negotiated or compromised.

The breaking point came on March 21, 2012 when the Defense Minister visited the Kati military camp in Bamako to defuse a protest the soldiers were planning for the following day. He was met with boos and stones were thrown at his car. When he came out of his car to speak, he addressed the soldiers in a superior, condescending manner, telling them that they had better fight or else. This was the spark that lit the powder keg. The soldiers became hostile, rushing and briefly detaining the surprised minister. His guards fired in the air to disperse the crowd of angry soldiers. He was later allowed to leave, but the damage had been done. The soldiers stormed the munitions reserves of the camp. They soon made their way through the city streets toward the presidential palace, situated atop a large plateau overlooking the city. When they arrived, they faced no resistance from the bodyguards. The president was nowhere to be found, having escaped with the help of the presidential guard. He went into hiding, eventually surfacing in neighboring Senegal where he was granted asylum. The soldiers looted the presidential palace, carrying off whatever they could get their hands on. Later the state broadcaster, ORTM, went off the air. When transmissions resumed, the military was in control and Malian democracy was officially over.

The MNLA took full advantage of the coup and swept across the northern portion of the country, capturing the three main urban areas of Kidal, Gao and Timbuktu. This coup was just the opportunity that they and their allies had been waiting for. The power vacuum in Bamako left the military in complete disarray. The fighting between the Malian army and the Tuareg rebels became bloodier. In February there were reports of a massacre of Malian troops, many of whom had their throats slit. Others were reportedly forced to dig their own graves before they were shot by the rebels. From the time of the first assaults in Menaka, Aguelhok and Tessalit on January 16th and 17th, to the fall of Ali Farka's beloved Niafunke on February 1st, to the capture of the three biggest cities in the region, the reports came through, one after another, burning like a brush fire in the dry season. By April 6th the Tuareg conquest of northern Mali was complete. Their declaration of independence was roundly rejected by its neighbors, the African Union, ECOWAS (Economic Community of West African states), the United Nations, France and other na-

7

tions. ECOWAS began preliminary preparations to send a force to Mali to re-take the north. The Malian army rejected this action and responded that any foreign troops on Malian soil would be treated as enemy invaders. In late April the army sent hundreds of soldiers to the Bamako-Senou airport to occupy the airport and await the arrival of ECOWAS forces. What began as a series of isolated rebel attacks in northern Mali, culminated in a coup d'etat and the frightening prospect of ECOWAS states fighting both the Malian army and the Tuareg rebels at the same time. Red-tape and bureaucratic wrangling between Mali's neighbors and the U.N. indefinitely delayed the invasion. Tensions cooled slightly over time. On April 6, 2012 the army made a show of conceding to a weak civilian government to avoid crippling sanctions from ECOWAS. However they retained considerable power and influence behind the scenes. On May 21st a mob stormed the presidential palace and attacked interim president Diouncounda Traore, beating him within an inch of his life. The soldiers and presidential guard stood by and watched. Many saw the interim civilian regime as too close to the old guard. Pro-military and civilian government sentiments divided many ordinary Malians. As a result of the continued political disunity in the capital city of Bamako, the Islamists' grip on the north tightened.

The government had long accused the rebels of being a front for AQIM, and it was said that elements of AQIM were present among the loose federation of fighters who accompanied the MNLA. Other, foreign groups such as Nigeria's Boko Haram ("western education is sin") were also on the scene to capitalize on the various opportunities that accompany extreme chaos. In reality, the ultimate agendas of each group differed greatly. The MNLA's stated focus was the liberation of the Azawad from the Republic of Mali. In Timbuktu one former army garrison was occupied by MNLA fighters while another garrison flew the black flag of Ansar Dine. Eventually Ansar Dine imposed sharia law on the town, banning alcohol, cigarettes and all music while enforcing the veiling of women. The marriage of convenience between the Islamists and the MNLA broke down. More blood was spilled. The secular Tuareg rebels were chased from the cities and town as the Islamists solidified their grip. They were joined by MUJAO (Movement for Oneness and Jihad in West Africa), a splinter of AQIM whose stated goals include the imposition of sharia law across a vast region of West Africa. A UNESCO world heritage site, Timbuktu is the home of many priceless manuscripts and ancient architecture. There are also numerous shrines to Sufi saints. Fighters from MUJAO and Ansar Dine desecrated several of these shrines by attacking the graves and smashing and burning the doors and windows that protect them. The pious worshippers assembled there could only look on in horror. Ansar Dine fighters told the local population that such shrines were 'haram' ("forbidden") in Islam, and that they would destroy all of them, saying, "Islam does not like it." Schools that had been closed were finally reopened, but any courses that did not adhere to Ansar Dine's myopic version of education were eliminated.

The authorities banned all music. The radio played only Koranic verses. Even cell phone ringtones were prohibited. It is a sad irony that in ancient days Timbuktu was a center of learning for the entire Islamic world, known for its sages, scholars and openness to the world. Under the foreign-imposed sharia law, Timbuktu became a shell of its former self, the scene of murder, rape, pillage and violence.

9

Hundreds of thousands fled from the region and public stonings, whippings and amputations for real or perceived violations of sharia law became commonplace. Mali experienced its worst crisis in more than fifty years. In January, 2013 French military forces began a three-month long war to evict the new lords of the desert. Though they were eventually successful in driving off or killing many of the foreign-backed jihadists, this only opened the door to an interminable guerrilla war fought with roadside bombs and surprise attacks. What was once thought to be an easy cleanup job turned out to be much harder. Could Mali turn into a quagmire like Vietnam was for the Americans or Afghanistan was for the Soviets? Only time will tell. It is not an exaggeration to say that all eyes are on this modern nation with an ancient pedigree. The country used to be a poster child for democracy in the region. Now it is the latest battleground and also the latest casualty in the global so-called 'War on Terror'.

ᚼ

It is 2002 and I am in Niafunke to record an album called "Mississippi to Mali", a collaboration with Ali Farka.

It is March, one of the hottest months of the year. One day I decide to take a walk around town after eating lunch. It is a dry, cloudless day. The unpaved streets explode in clouds of fine dust every time a car, motorcycle or donkey cart passes by. I can taste it as it mixes with the scent of cooking from unseen, mud-brick courtyards and distant brush fires. I see the tents of local Tuaregs, their occupants resting languidly in the shade. A small assortment of goats, chickens and donkeys amble about, going nowhere fast. It is as if they too are trying to preserve their energy as they navigate the desert sand under the hot sun. I walk into a small store owned by Tuareg merchants. There are two young men inside, one behind the counter of the sparsely decorated interior. One is dressed in the traditional blue turban and long boubou, while the other wears a western collared shirt and pants. They look like they are related, with their olive skin, straight brown hair and serious, somber faces. This store is housed inside an old shipping container. I look on the walls and see the basic staples of canned foods, personal care products, simple household items and the ubiquitous boxes of imported Chinese 'gunpowder' green tea. There is even a brand, "Tuareg" which comes in a small, green, cube-shaped box. The drawing on the outside depicts two blue-turbaned men mounted on camels with a panorama of endless dunes stretching out behind them. On the box it says "qualite superior...produit de chine." The young men give an understated response to my greetings, their eyes showing no sign of pretense or smile. They would win any staring contest with their stoic demeanor. They are matter-of-fact in their interactions, showing no outward motion or unnecessary chatter.

Looking me over, they ask where I am from. I tell them I live in Virginia, USA and they are cordial but uninterested. There is one long swathe of midnight-black fabric. They catch me looking at it with some interest. I don't even have to point to it. Within seconds it is unfolded before me to examine and I begin to negotiate a price. Seeing that I am a foreigner, they give an extremely high first price, an amount that is much more than the average Malian would imagine paying. I do my best to bring them down, with little success. These are typical of the turbans seen throughout the desert, worn not only by Tuaregs but also Songhai, Peul, Bambara and other ethnic groups for

11

protection against the harsh elements and for warmth in the cold desert night. As we negotiate back and forth I see another advantage to the turbans: they cover the entire face except the eyes, hiding emotion and expression. This makes the deal less friendly and more like straight business.

In Africa, negotiation is a game played every day, like poker. Also like poker, the ability to hide one's emotions during the game is a prime advantage. I haven't made any real progress negotiating with these stone-faced brethren. As I am about to pay, I hear a familiar voice at the doorway. It is Ali Farka. He is all smiles and warmth and greets us all. He enters the small, dusty shop, immediately buys the black turban and gives it to me as a gift. His very presence has changed the mood inside this tiny shop. I see that the Tuareg brother wearing the turban has unwrapped it, showing his face. Both he and his brother are now grinning happily. I have never seen such a quick transition from stone-cold poker face to warm smiles as I did on that hot day. That day I learned that there was something special about Ali Farka Toure in the way he could make people comfortable. He did it with humor, simplicity, kindness, and a spirit of comraderie that you could hear in his voice when he spoke. He was both noble and a man of the people. He didn't like fancy things nor was he ostentatious. He lived a simple life and he worked hard for his family, his culture, his community and his nation. The proof is in his music and the power of the words that he sings.

I recall a hot day in the courtyard of the Hotel Campement, owned by Ali and operated by his cousin Berte Toure. I am here with a recording engineer who has traveled with me from Virginia. We sit on white plastic chairs listening to hip-hop on a portable cassette player with three young Bambara men from Niafunke. There is a doorway to the courtyard of the hotel in front of which people on the street would pass to and fro. A few passersby stop and reverse to get another curious look at these two Black dreads from the USA bobbing their heads in unison with the local youth. The song, "Oochie Wally", by Nas' brother Jungle, is a hit in the US. But hearing it in a remote desert town on the banks of the river Niger redefines the meaning of 'hit'. The doorway is like a window to the outside world of the dusty streets of Niafunke. Watching the doorway as the world passes by gives us a brief snapshot in time as people, goats, donkeys and chickens walk back and forth. Small brown and multi-colored margoya lizards scurry across the dry ground and on the walls, stopping to do push-ups as they inflate air sacs in their throats. A slightly-built Tuareg man wearing flip-flops and a blue turban with traditional shirt and pants stops in the doorway and then comes back a few minutes later to get a second look. He walks into the courtyard, greets everyone with one, quiet word, and sits down. This Tuareg brother is checking us out.

The desert sun beams down on us all. Intense brown eyes look us over from behind the Turban that cover his young but weathered face. He sits quietly for awhile, observing the strangers who have come from so far away. Then he begins to bob his head to the boom-bap just like the rest of us. No manual necessary. After a while he says another quiet word and exits the doorway through which he had come. Hip-hop is big everywhere you go in Mali, just as it has taken over the rest of the globe. Here, this Black art revolution from the south Bronx is loved by the youth like a long lost twin brother. Africa is the cradle of

13

the beat and the spoken word, and hip-hop is but the latest manifestation of the ancient tradition of rhythm and rhyme. It comes from a different recent history, as the culmination of Africans' exodus from the Jim Crow and lynchings of the the southern states to the discrimination, crime, and economic desolation of the inner cities. But it can still come home to Africa and be recognized like a prodigal son. Africans recognize that Black music is African at its core; they love the music regardless of style or national origin. In the near future this music will be under attack in the land of its birth.

Ali had a special affinity for Bambara music. I learned Bajourou, a traditional Bambara song, from him. He taught me another song during my brief time with him, 'Rokie', a traditional Tuareg tune that he explained is also a dance. Ali knew his own culture and he celebrated other Malian cultures through music. Like his namesake the donkey, he carried many others through life. This explains why the two Tuaregs in the shop smiled so widely. He not only treated people right, he patronized their businesses. He helped as many people in his community as he could, regardless of origin. Whoever you were -- Tuareg, Bambara, African-American, European -- Ali Farka Toure made you know that you shared something in common with him.

Before war came to northern Mali, Niafunke was alive with the sounds of music and dancing. Wedding celebrations were common. During the Islamist occupation, musicians who had not left Niafunke and the other cities and towns across the north lived in fear. The Islamists routinely destroyed their instruments and threatened to cut out the tongues of singers. Many musicians fled to Bamako, but their existence there was meager since the tourists

14

had stopped coming. The entire culture and way of life was under attack from within by people who had been indoctrinated against African culture by outside ideas and foreign sponsors. Mali's tolerant Sufi faith was being supplanted by a rigid, violent culture that masquerades as true Islam. Foreigners were regularly kidnapped for ransom. The islamists also profited handsomely from the arms and narcotics (cocaine, heroin) that were moved along the ancient trans-Saharan trade routes under their control. Reprisal attacks against both Tuaregs and Arabs increased, as they were seen to be in collaboration with the different Tuareg and Arab islamist groups who had recently lost their foothold in the desert. Many Malian Tuareg and Arab men left the country with their families to live in refugee camps in Mauritania and other neighboring countries.

Ali Farka would surely be horrified to see the fragmentation of the once unified nation. A Muslim and a lover of African culture, he would have spoken against the madness and violence that has infected his homeland. His music would have educated others against the vice, abuse and bloodshed that accompanied the rebel occupation. Through his music and his life, Ali Farka Toure laid a path of peace with respect for all. The hope for Mali is that enough people will follow this path to make a real difference in the lives of the people.

THE ROAD TO NIAFUNKE

"However far the stream flows, it never forgets its source."
- Yoruba proverb

*M*arch 3, 2006. It is a hot, dry Friday in Bamako. Samba Toure is paying a visit to Ali Farka Toure at his home in the Lafiabougou neighborhood. The red dust is heavy in the air as the daily soccer game rages on in front of the large white house tucked behind the white exterior walls of the compound. A few players have genuine soccer shoes but the rest of them play in plastic sandals. The half-acre of earth serves as a parking lot, praying ground, meeting place and playing field, depending on the time of day. Africa does not run on the European clock, but everything runs on time just the same. There is 'black man time' and there is 'white man time.' Five times every day the call to prayer is announced by the muezzin from the nearby mosque. In between these times the field serves its other purposes. People travel to and fro on the unpaved road in various European and Japanese cars and trucks, competing with the many mopeds for a share of the narrow streets and wide boulevards. Chickens and goats walk about, picking at whatever they can find in the small piles of refuse at the edges of the playing/praying field. The

16

scooter riders and motorists who pass by cover their noses and mouths with bandanas or the common airline sleeping masks to keep the dust out. Bamako is a noisy and polluted metropolis that never seems to stop. It feels like a world away from the northern part of the country, with its vast, quiet expanses of Sahel and the endless sands of the Sahara. Northern Mali is the ancient land of the Songhai.

Ali's house in Bamako is like a Songhai oasis in the middle of Bamako, in southern Mali. Slender young men of varying height, relations of Ali's family whom he has taken in, sit outside and take turns preparing small pots of green tea with mint leaves and sugar. To an observer the amount of sugar dissolved into the tea would seem to be enough to induce diabetic shock. They will drink the strong, dark brew in shot glasses and then light more coals in the miniature stove to start the whole process over again. Someone gives a small boy 250 CFA (about $1US) to walk to the store and buy small plastic bags of green tea, cane sugar and a handful of fresh mint leaves. The tea is tightly packed and dried into little black balls resembling gunpowder. Like Ali, Samba is also Songhai. Not quite six feet tall, he is a stocky man with a round, youthful face and a deep chocolate complexion. He is in his mid -thirties. A fierce guitarist and vocalist, his sound has gradually evolved from his interpretation of the highly-danceable Congolese Soukous music that he once played for Bamako audiences to a full embrace of the gritty, hard-driving traditional music of the desert north. Ali Farka was the reason for this transformation. Early on, he pushed Samba to explore and express himself in the musical language of his roots. The young man from Timbuktu listened to his elder's advice, and soon he was traveling with 'ton-ton' (uncle) around the world. He and the other young lions such as Ali's son, Vieux Far-

17

ka, Ali's nephew, Afel Boucoum and Ali Magassa will carry on the legacy of Songhai desert blues into the future. This particular Friday, Ali is very sick and near the end of his battle with bone cancer. He can't walk anymore and the pain won't go away. Once towering and muscular, he is now extremely thin and his skin is the color of ashes. Ali is dying. Still, his voice is strong, strong enough that those who call him on the phone can't tell the difference. His sickness is evident in the way he sits in a chair, almost as if he is propped up. But put a guitar in his hands and the weakness seems to disappear. He will play guitar almost to the very end of his life. Samba tells Ali that he must go back to his home in Timbuktu. Ali says he will be traveling too. "I am going to Niafunke Wednesday." Samba asks, "But how are you going to get there? You're not well yet." Ali says, "It's over." Surprised, Samba says, "What?" Ali waves his hand as if to say 'never mind'. "It's ok...anyway I am going to Niafunke." Samba asks if he will fly or take the road. Ali says no, he will take the road. Saturday, Sunday and Monday passes and Ali's condition continues to worsen.

During the night, Samba, Oumar, and the family see that he isn't doing very well so they put him in a car and take him to the hospital. He won't make it. He dies in the car on the way to the hospital. It is around four o'clock on a Tuesday morning. They take his body to a morgue where it will stay until the following day, the same day that Ali told Samba that he would leave Bamako for Niafunke. On this day, the Malian government makes arrangements to fly the corpse to Niafunke. There are three planes at the Bamako airport, but there are no flights due to a severe windstorm. There are thousands of people – family, friends, fellow musicians, dignitaries and onlookers – assembled at

Bamako airport. They wait an hour but it is obvious that there will be no flying today. The haze is blinding, with the blowing sand that stings the skin like a sandblaster. Finally the Prime Minister says, "It's finished. Bring the vehicles." The convoy leaves the airport for the two day-long voyage to Niafunke. Samba remembers that Farka told him on Friday that he would go to Niafunke on this very day, by road. True to his prophecy, Ali's body is driven to his beloved hometown. Speaking quietly as he recollects, Samba says, "So every time...since Farka passed away until today, thirty minutes have not passed without thinking about him. I only listen to his music. Coming here in my car, it was his music I was listening to, his cd. So we will never forget Ali Farka. That's it." It is dark now. The evening soccer game and the call to prayer have long since ended. Normally smiling and laughing, Oumar and his nephew Samba are now both somber as they think about the passing of a great man. Tears do not visibly flow, but they are below the surface, like water running under the desert, searching for a spring.

Oumar Toure first met Ali in nineteen sixty-five and began playing with him regularly in nineteen eighty-nine. Of all Ali's friends and family, it is perhaps this quiet-spoken conga player from Dire, a town in the Timbuktu region on the banks of the Niger, who knows him best. Oumar accompanies Ali Farka from the beginning of his professional touring career right up until his passing. Their relationship is deep. He is Ali's employee, conga player, confidante, intermediary, brother and friend. He is always by

19

his side. In his final days, Ali tells Oumar matter-of-factly, "I must go home to die. No problem." There is a television in the room. It is playing one of Ali's songs. Though he is near death and rail-thin, his spirit is still strong. Recognizing his music, Ali looks at Oumar with a sparkle in his eye and exclaims, "Hey!" snapping his fingers and pointing towards the television. The medicine that he is taking often causes him to lapse into a deep sleep. Sitting with Ali, Oumar tells him, "I need to go." Ali opens his eyes and laughs. "Ha! Ha! Sit down." Either Ali isn't hearing him, or doesn't want to hear what his old friend is telling him. Oumar says, "I need to go back home [to his village]. It's been a long time since I have seen my family. I've got to go. I told you that I would never leave you. I can't leave you, but there are some things that are obligatory. I have my little children." Ali says, "Ok. We will make a benediction to say bon voyage." This is the last time Oumar sees his brother, benefactor, patron, employer and friend Ali Farka Toure alive.

Everyone in the village of Dire knows that Oumar's wife is a seer. If she sees something in her dreams, it will come true or you will hear about it through someone else. Though he is happy to see his family and sleep in his own bed, Oumar is restless. Every time he would begin to dream, Farka would appear to him in the dream, saying, "Get up." He rises quickly the next morning and hears his wife telling him, "You need to say your prayers. I saw something yesterday in a dream that I can't believe." Oumar says, "Oh really?" Just then, there is somebody knocking at the door. Oumar says, "What is it?" He opens the door and sees his elder brother standing there. Someone has telephoned to say that Ali had just died, and that the body would come to Niafunke on Tuesday or Wednesday.

Oumar's brother has already packed his bags and is leaving. Knowing the truth, but not wanting to believe, Oumar asks him, "Is he dead?" Recalling the shock, he said, "From the first word, I couldn't see anything. One would say that I had become blind." Immediately he takes a car and travels to Niafunke to be with the family.

Ali's body arrives the day after Oumar reaches Niafunke. He is given a state funeral attended by the President and all the government ministers. Oumar remembers that it seemed as if all the musicians in Mali were there: international stars such as Toumani Diabate, Djelimady Tounkara, Salif Keita, Keletigui Diabate. Many other notable artists have come to share their grief with thousands of everyday Malians. People have come from as far away as Europe and the United States to witness Jahtigui's (Father Lion's) final voyage. "Everybody was crying. Everybody was crying. Ooh la la…that was a day. I had never seen that, no one had ever seen that in Mali. They went all the way to Niafunke." Niafunke is 850 kilometers (530 miles) from Bamako. In a country with few paved highways, such a journey can take two days or more. The thousands who descended upon the small town are a testament to the love for the man and his music. This giant has fallen asleep, but he has left big footsteps to fill.

Ali leaves eleven children and three wives behind to mourn his passing. Oumar says he is worried about Arama, Ali's young daughter who was very close to her father. She and her brothers Vieux and Hasay have the same mother. All three of them have the deep-black complexion of their father."Every time you can see her next to her father. Even if her father is on the telephone she will go like this [pulls his ear] to hear. She was very dear to

21

her father. So when I came to Niafunke, she came to me and asked, 'Baba, ca va?' ("Papa, how is it going?") There weren't even any plans made yet. It was the very same day [that Ali had died]." This same young girl is now a beautiful woman, busy cooking in the courtyard and tending to the household duties. She and her brothers will carry the legacy on into the future.

THE SOURCE

"Work on your reputation until it is established; when it is established it will work for you."

- Tunisian proverb

$\mathcal{A}$li Farka Toure was a giant among men. His music, his generosity, and his work ethic loom large, even after his passing. 'The blues,' is what many Westerners would call this music that is drenched in trance-like tonalities, wails and moans, and a heavy, incessant rhythm. This desert music - sung in several languages indigenous to Mali: Songhai, Peul, Bambara, Tamasheck -- predates the blues by more than a thousand years. Contrary to the twisted imaginations of many western historians, Africans did not come to the New World devoid of culture. The musical and cultural traditions of the Motherland are the seeds that gave birth to the blues. Transformed in the crucible of the horrors of enslavement, segregation, discrimination and Jim Crow, the blues is the story of Black people in North America after Africa. Blues as well as nineteenth century Black banjo music, ragtime, jazz, funk, soul and R&B are all styles rooted in the pentatonic scales and blue notes found in the musical traditions of the Mali empire.

Djeli (griots) are the keepers of this rich musical tradition, which is at least 1,500 years old. In addition to drums, the kora, ballophone and guitar, many djeli play the ngoni, a four to nine-stringed, oblong-shaped lute covered in goatskin. Traditionally its strings were made from gut but in modern times nylon fishing line is used. There are several sizes or types of ngoni and they each have a distinctive sound. Although variations of this ancestor of the banjo are found throughout Africa, all have their origins in the ancient civilizations of the Nile Valley. The djeli are the living memory of the Mali Empire and Mandinka culture. The word literally means "blood." Indeed, one does not become a djeli but rather one must be born into it. It is in the blood. Djelis are found in a wide swath across West Africa, with each ethnic group having their own particular name for this hereditary caste. This ancient profession includes advising kings and accompanying them into battle, deciding proper protocol in royal and noble households, recording the history and genealogy of the people, mediation and arbitration of disputes and contracts, bestowing blessings at marriages, births, baptisms, funerals, as well as playing music. Though they are renowned for their musical talents, djelis are first and foremost masters of the spoken word. It is said that a djeli is unable to lie, and they remember everything. Though he was not a djeli, Ali Farka Toure played with all the great djeli ngoni players of his era. This deep familiarity with the ngoni was a cornerstone of his guitar style.

Though they are indispensable to Malian culture, the caste does not enjoy a lofty status in Malian society. The term can be employed with derision; indeed, non-djelis have been heard to refer to them as slaves. Perhaps this is because of their perennial service to the upper classes.

These men and women (women are called djelimousso - lit. 'woman djeli') commonly require payment for their services and the blessings that they bring. Upon hearing the emotive praises of the djeli set to song, the rich are known to gift them with money, cars, even entire homes. Some djeli are cosmopolitan in their outlook and financially successful, while others are more provincial and live quite meagerly. There is also the stereotype of the djeli as one who lives perpetually with his hand extended, surviving off of the generosity of the noble classes. This caricature is ever ready to whip out the appropriate songs in the presence of the noble in hopes of getting some quick money. However, this is seldom the reality. In fact, not all djeli play music. Many become teachers, intellectuals and writers, while some follow other careers. Indeed, the varied talents required of the djeli -- conflict mediation, household protocol, genealogy, history, oratory, baptism, marriage and music -- make them suited to succeed in many fields. No matter what profession one chooses, the designation of djeli can never be shaken. The knowledge of a djeli is held in such high esteem that when a djeli dies people say it is like a library has burned to the ground.

Ali Ibrahim "Farka" Toure was born in 1939 in Kanau, a small village on the banks of the Niger. Like many Africans of his generation born without an official birth certificate, he didn't know his exact birthday. His father was a noble of the Songhai ethnic group known as the Arma, while his mother was a member of the Peul ethnic group. When he was still an infant his father died while serving in the French Foreign Legion. Soon afterwards, the family moved south to nearby Niafunke, an outpost several hours drive from the legendary Timbuktu. He was the only surviving son of ten siblings. As is the custom

25

in many parts of Africa, a surviving child is often given a strange name. "Farka" translates as "donkey" an animal known for its stubborness and tenacity. His elders initially discouraged him from playing music, an activity of the djeli and thus judged to be below his status. The renowned ngoni player and djeli Bassekou Kouyate explains that before Mali's independence the caste system was the order of the day. Every family had their profession and their place in society. This was the tradition. According to Bassekou, the word 'les artistes' did not even exist in Mali, since only those whose families were djeli could practice the art of djeliya. Nobles recoiled at the idea of their daughters or sons marrying beneath their status. Yet every noble since ancient times has relied on the advice of their djeli and have respected their authority in various matters. They are indispensable. Despite all of this, when Ali Farka's family realized his ambitions to play music, they were not pleased. He was one of the first Malian 'artistes' -- those who loved music but were prohibited to play it because of their caste -- but who nonetheless defied tradition and opened the doors for anyone who wanted to play music regardless of caste. The aspirations of this new generation of artists led them to defy the expectations of tradition. Where music had previously been the sole domain of the djeli, these artists laid the foundation for a music industry where participation was based on talent rather than caste.

Though he was born into Islam, he also recognized the indigenous Songhai belief system that is closely connected with the powerful, life-giving waters of the Joliba (Niger) River. Ali Farka Toure was a 'child of the river'. Beneath the mighty river is a realm of powerful spirits known as Ghimbala. These spirits are known to manifest in male and female forms, each with their own history, character, symbolism and ritual objects. They have power over both the temporal and spiritual world. Those who are able to communicate with them are called 'children of the river'. In fact, Ali's grandmother Kounandi Samba was a renowned priestess of the Ghimbala famous for her deep connection to these river spirits.

He farmed throughout his childhood and later apprenticed as a tailor. During this time he was exposed to Ghimbala music ceremonies that were common in the many small villages along the banks of the Joliba. He spent many hours listening to the sacred musicians as they performed on the favored instruments of the Ghimbala: the njarka (one-stringed violin), the djerkel (one-stringed lute) and the ngoni. He was deeply affected by the music of the many djeli who would come to play for his father The influence of all these musicians and singers had a profound and lasting effect on his music. Being surrounded by so much music, it became his passion, even though he faced constant discouragement from his elders. They thought it was pure folly for a boy to dream about music instead of doing the hard work in the fields like every one else. His dogged determination led him to make a djerkel, his first instrument which he played in secret with his friends. Though as an adult he came to be respected as a traditionalist, the very act of a noble child playing music was extremely contrary to the tradition in which he was raised. It was an act of pure defiance. "I am not a griot, and I am not a slave. It is forbidden in a noble family to be an artist."

When his elders found out that Ali had begun to play, they took drastic measures to stop him. They sent him off to a traditional healer in a neighboring village, who bound his arms and subjected him to a year of treatments intended to extinguish his desire to play music. However, when he returned to Niafunke his communication with the spirits was even stronger. When his grandmother passed away he was deterred from becoming a priest to the Ghimbala. Later in life he was quoted as saying, "Because of Islam, I don't want to practice this type of thing too much. These spirits can be good to you or bad so I just sing about them, but it's our culture, we can't pass it by." Ali always kept his njarka by his side and often listened to recordings of the spirit music he knew from his early childhood. Stubborn as his namesake, Ali did not give up his love of music, despite his family's constant efforts to force him to yield to tradition. Eventually, his elders accepted that he would not be dissuaded from the path he had chosen for himself. Ali once said, "God gives us all ambitions, and He gives to those who are righteous." As John Lee Hooker once sang in his song, 'Boogie Chillen', "...let the boy boogie. It's in him, and it's got to come out." They let Ali play his music.

His twin passions were music and farming. However, he identified himself as a farmer, first and foremost. Those who knew him as a young man say he was born in the dirt. Throughout his life, he never stopped farming, taking only the necessary time to tour. But he always came home to the land. He was a son of the soil. As a young man Ali worked as a mechanic, chauffeur and river ambulance pilot, which led to him traveling widely within Mali. He also continued to play music in spirit ceremonies, accompanying singers. "I got to know music and to love it through so many heroes who passed on and who continue

28

to live on the earth, because history remains. So it gave me the opportunity to get to know the culture of this music, its biography, legends and history." By the time he was in his early twenties he spoke seven Malian languages fluently and was a master of the ngoni, njarka and the bamboo flute as played by the Peul. He sang in all the languages of the region - Peul, Bamana, Dogon, Songhai, Zarma, Bozo and Tamasheck - though the majority of his repertoire was in Songhai and Peul. In 1956 he saw a performance of the National Ballet of Guinea featuring the legendary Malinke virtuoso guitarist Fodeba Keita. "That's when I swore I would become a guitarist. I didn't know his guitar (style) but I liked it a lot. I felt I had as much music as him and that I could translate it." Ali began to adapt the traditional music he knew from childhood to the guitar. Soon he added percussion, drums, and accordion to the arsenal of instruments he already played. It was his intimate familiarity with traditional music and instruments that made him such a formidable force on the guitar. He didn't play guitar music but rather traditional music on the guitar. He learned how to mimic the sounds of traditional instruments in a way that transcended the guitar itself.

In the early sixties Ali represented Niafunke at the Semaine National de La Jeunesse (National Youth Week), a bi-annual celebration of arts and sport that featured troupes from each of the six regions of Mali. Starting in 1962 he co-led the Niafunke district troupe with another musician, a young man named Harbarie Labere. In addition to singing, composing and playing music, Ali rehearsed the troupe of one hundred and seventeen singers and dancers for the event. He also won many athletic prizes, saying, "I did this so my village wouldn't win zero. I'm very patriotic!" During these years he accompanied various singers as well as leading his own small group. This ensemble played traditional Malian repertoire as well as adaptations of other music such as Afro-Cuban selections sung in Songhai. In 1968 he was selected along with the legendary ballophone player Keletigui Diabate and the virtuoso guitarist Djelimady Tounkara to represent Mali at an international festival of the arts in Sofia, Bulgaria. This was his first appearance overseas. Their repertoire of traditional music with Ali on guitar, flute, djerkel and njarka was well received. He bought his first guitar while in Bulgaria on April 21st, 1968. Around this time he first heard the music of Wilson Pickett, James Brown, Otis Redding, Jimmy Smith and Albert King, in which he said he recognized so much of his own musical traditions. But the one whose music struck him as being most similar to his own was the legendary John Lee Hooker. Upon hearing this music for the first time, he was amazed and thought to himself that "this music was taken from here."

Throughout the 1970's Ali worked in Bamako at Radio Mali as an assistant sound engineer to Aboubacar Traore. He also briefly played in its orchestra which was ultimately disbanded in 1973. Everyone in Mali who had a radio soon became familiar with Ali Farka Toure's voice and guitar. It was during this time that he began to send recordings of his broadcasts to the Son Afric record label in Paris. The first Ali Farka Toure album was released a few months later, featuring Ali on guitar and Nassourou Sarre on ngoni. Six more albums were released in this same manner, with tracks from the first five of these being released as the CD 'Radio Mali' on the World Circuit record label. He did not see any royalties from his releases with Son Afric, which later explained his initial unhappiness when his son Vieux decided he also wanted to play music for a living. Nevertheless, Ali's reputation steadily grew throughout the 1970's as he perfected the adaptation of Songhai, Peul and Tamasheck repertoire and style to the guitar. Eschewing the commercial route, Ali remained a steadfast traditionalist, continuing to sing songs which spoke to the realities of life in Mali, the land, the river and the spirits. By 1986 his music began to attract serious attention from radio d.j's in London, but little was known about him in England as the albums did not have liner notes. This led to Anne Hunt from World Circuit traveling to Bamako to try and find this mysterious farmer/musician from Niafunke. An announcement was made on Radio Mali asking Ali to please come and present himself. Though he had since moved back to Niafunke, it just so happened that he was visiting Bamako that same day. He came to the radio station to meet the English woman who had traveled so far to find him. Soon afterwards an invitation was extended for him to perform in the U.K. in 1987, marking the first time since playing in Bulgaria in 1968 that he would perform outside of Africa. His first recordings outside of the African market were released by World Circuit that same year, which were greeted with unparalleled enthusiasm by British audiences. Afterwards he toured Europe, U.S.A., Canada, Brazil and Japan while continuing to record five more albums for World Circuit, including The River, The Source and Talking Timbuktu, the GRAMMY award-winning collaboration with Ry Cooder. Ali Farka Toure had fully arrived on the world stage.

Toward the end of his life, he retired from touring so that he could devote more time to his community and his farm. In fact, when World Circuit wanted to record Ali for his album, 'Niafunke', he made them come to him. British recording engineer Jerry Boys (Buena Vista Social Club)

31

and World Circuit record company head Nick Gold converted an abandoned agricultural school into a field studio. Ever a son of the soil, the recording sessions had to accommodate Ali's work on the farm, as the crops always came first. The album, Niafunke, was released in 1999. Music was still his love, but his hometown was now his main focus. At this stage of his life he rarely played live and took a long hiatus from recording, turning down numerous offers to perform. In 2004 he accepted an invitation to play at the small Privas festival in southern France, donating his entire fee to development projects in his hometown. That same year he was elected mayor of Niafunke. In 2005 he traveled to Belgium, playing his first major concert in five years, where he performed with the celebrated kora master Toumani Diabate which was received with rapturous delight by both fans and press.

In the same year the first of three records recorded at Bamako's Hotel Mande was released, In the Heart of the Moon, featuring collaborations with Toumani Diabate. The record received a GRAMMY award, making Ali the only African to receive the award twice. Ali followed up this release with an extensive European tour with Toumani and the renowned ngoni player Bassekou Kouyate, who collaborated with Ali on Savane, the third album in the Hotel Mande series. During this time he also entered a London recording studio with Toumani and the Cuban bassist Orlando 'Cachaito' Lopez. For the remainder of his life Ali worked tirelessly for sanitation, electrical and irrigation projects to benefit the town. It was often said that Ali accounted for over 80% of the local economy. He owned hotels and real estate (in Niafunke and in Bamako), several transport vehicles, a garage, thousands of cattle, and a vast farm. He used the proceeds from his music for the betterment of his community. It was quite appropriate that a man upon whom so many relied for their daily bread would be named 'donkey'. "But let me make one thing clear" he said, "I'm the donkey that nobody climbs upon!" He carried many heavy loads in life, without complaint. He would not live to see the release of Savane, passing away just weeks after receiving the GRAMMY and approving the final master. He died in Bamako on March 7th, 2006 finally succumbing to the bone cancer which he had been fighting for several years. He was 66 years old. He is buried in Niafunke.

He loved the blues, but often said that his music began long before the blues was born. Many European and American writers were eager to give all the credit to the John Lee Hooker records Ali had heard after his style and approach to music had already fully manifested. He was definitely influenced by the blues he heard on records but he was secure in his musical identity. He often recalled his surprise the first time he heard Hooker, saying, "Where did they get this culture? This is something that belongs to us!" As for the blues, Ali said, "to me blue is just a color. My music came long before the blues was born." When he drove across the vast desert of northern Mali in his Land Rover, Ali's stereo blasted the music of Ray Charles, Otis Redding, Bobby Blue Bland and other blues and soul artists whom he recognized as his musical kinsmen. It didn't matter to him that much of the English that they sung in was unintelligible to him. Upon learning of the passing of John Lee Hooker in 2001, Ali extended his heartfelt condolences. He knew that they belonged to the same musical family, rooted in the civilizations of ancient Africa. He celebrated the African root of the blues as common knowledge, though many western audiences did not see the connection so clearly. Many thought it simply impossible that such a long history lay behind the music. Implicit in this idea is that Africans came to the West with no cultural traditions. Ali knew that Black American music has deep roots extending into the ancient empires of West Africa from which Black Americans' ancestors were torn. He spoke about it often. Just as European and other immigrant populations in North America persevered and further developed the music of their ancestors, so was the case with Africans in the Americas. Toumani Diabate once said "You can take people...you can take off his clothes, you can take off his shoes, you can take his name and give him another name.... the only thing that you can't ever take from him is his culture." Ali Farka Toure represented the missing link between African music and Black American music. To know his music is to know the source.

BLUES ON THE JOLIBA

"When it comes to blues, he exposed the real source of things. His music wasn't just for Mali or for Africa, but for the whole world."

- Toumani Diabate

*I*t is July 2001, my first meeting with Ali Farka. I am in Mali to film a documentary with a New York city crew dispatched by Martin Scorsese for PBS, 'Feel Like Going Home." The film documents the African origins of the blues, beginning in Mississippi and culminating with a visit to Niafunke, Ali's home in the northern desert on the banks of the Niger. Our flight to the north is arranged through African Airlines, a charter based in the capital of Bamako and owned by a Pakistani brother and sister who once lived in Idi Amin's Uganda before being forced into exile. The flight crew is Ukrainian, which explains what an old Russian twin-engine plane is doing here in West Africa. As we taxi down the runway the engines roar while the aircraft rattles and shakes its way slowly into the dusty atmosphere above. I watch the outlines of people working the fields below shrink and then finally disappear into the haze and heat of the Sahel.

35

There is no separation between the cabin and the cockpit, and the passengers can see straight through the front windshield. On the noisy flight north I follow the Niger river as it cuts a watery path through the dry expanses of treeless desert. I see bushes broken up by the occasional tracks in the sand. We are between the arid sahel and the deep desert of the Sahara. It is hard to imagine that a few centuries ago there were actually trees here, before the creeping Sahara choked them out in a slow avalanche of sand. Over time, deforestation has also contributed to the gradual advance of the desert. A few thousand years ago, even the mighty Sahara itself was once verdant and fertile, with lakes and rivers throughout. Now it is a vast ocean of shifting sands. Buried in its depths are the remains of ancient empires, waiting to be discovered. There are also oil and minerals, which makes it very attractive to wealthy Western nations caught up in the race for resources.

The vastness of the land makes it impossible to secure. Everybody knew that the government never had enough resources to fully secure the northern part of the country. How can one of the poorest nations on the planet securely maintain such enormous borders? Columbian drug cartels and other organized criminals have seized upon the opportunity and are running a pipeline to Europe right though northern Mali. Who could know that eleven years later, northern Mali would be shorn away from the southern half by Qatari-financed Algerian, Tuareg, and a mob of West African religious zealots who live to destroy the local culture and impose their brand of sharia law? There are almost no roads visible from this height, 10,000 feet above. It is desert as far as the eye can see. I try to doze off, but the roaring of the antiquated, soviet-made engines keep me awake. The pilot asks the cinematographer to come up to the cockpit. He tells him to take the wheel and gives him an impromptu flight lesson. After a few minutes he hands control of the plane back to the pilot and sits down. Now it's my turn. I sit down in the co-pilot seat, the pilot grinning next to me. Looking through the windshield I see endless white clouds. I take the wheel and he motions for me to turn it slightly, which I do. I feel a little tentative, this being my first time behind the wheel of a plane. The view is overwhelming, just clouds and haze. Smiling widely now, he motions for me to turn the wheel more. I hesitate. He chuckles and turns the wheel on his side of the cockpit back and forth with enough force to make the plane rock and bounce. This is all a big joke to him. The assistant producer, seated in back, yells out. She is afraid. We all are.

The pilot laughs happily for a few more seconds and then steadies the wheel. To everyone's relief, the rickety old plane stops rocking. He is the only one laughing. The passengers calm down and soon we are making our descent towards Niafunke, on the banks of the muddy river Niger. As we get closer to the ground I can see the flat, low rooftops of the mud brick buildings with zinc roofs. Adobe comes to mind. We land at the airport, a dry, sandy plain with no asphalt in sight. A lone windsock catches the sweltering breeze. The sun is almost blinding in the 110 degree heat. The terrain is flat, vanishing into the dusty haze of the distant desert. A couple of small, mud brick buildings are situated at the edge of the landing area, their zinc roofs shining in the bright sunlight. I can barely see a man in a long dark boubou and a turban trodding in the sand toward the distant horizon, walking stick in hand. A mirage shimmers over the vastness beyond.

As I descend from the aircraft, Ali approaches the plane. He is smiling blackness, the epitome of nobility, resplendent in a sky blue boubou. "This is my people! You are in the bend of the Niger, in the fertile land on the banks of the Niger River, which we are very proud of." He places his open palm on his chest for emphasis. "You are welcome here, welcome." He grabs my hand and leads me over to a crowd of children. I am introduced in Songhai, which he translates into French so that I can understand him. As he speaks, his eyes radiate as if they have been soaking up the desert sun for an eternity. "He is our acquaintance, our brother, our foreigner, our friend and our guest," he says to the children and the townspeople who are gathered here. There is a round of applause and I shake hands with the children.

They are amazed by this dreadlocked newcomer and surround me to get a closer look. I am as black as they are, but clearly unlike any African they have seen. They smile with curiosity in their eyes, taking me in. I try speaking to a few of them in French, but this is futile. As a whole, Malians hold fast to their culture and language, and even though French is the administrative language in many quarters, many children do not learn it until they go to school. Many adults never need to use this foreign tongue with any regularity, though they may know as many as seven languages fluently. The children look at me and smile and laugh. I hear the musical cadence of the Songhai tongue all around me. I don't understand the words, but the rhythm, the warmth of the people and the place make it feel like home. Looking at the people I see relatives and friends' faces. There is a strong feeling of familiarity, like an enormous family reunion. I am new to this place, but I have been here before.

We climb into Ali's white Landcruiser with him at the wheel. Soon we are bouncing across the sand towards the center of town and the Hotel Campement, our accommodations during our stay here. He owns the hotel. He pops one of several tapes into the cassette player and turns the volume up. We hear Bobby Blue Bland, Ray Charles, Otis Redding. I am a little surprised, expecting to hear ancient strains of traditional Songhai music or the deep desert blues he is known for. It is clear from looking at the old, dusty tapes strewn about the vehicle that this is not just for my benefit. This is what he listens to all the time. The music plays as a soundtrack to my first impressions of Niafunke and its narrow, sandy streets bordered by walled compounds on either side. Women walk with babies strapped to their backs, loads balanced on their heads.

Their posture is perfect as they glide along nobly, going about their day. Stoic and turbaned Tuaregs amble by in small groups. Their brown faces are covered by their turbans to protect against the harsh sun and ubiquitous dust. It is the dry season and sandstorms are common. The dust pervades everything, everywhere, like so much reddish-brown powdered sugar. Ali honks his horn and waves as we speed along, avoiding the many potholes in the road. We pass men driving donkey carts, while goats stroll about. Some donkeys linger by the roadside, their long ears standing at attention. Occasionally a scrawny chicken scratches in the sand at the side of the road. When we arrive at the hotel we are greeted by a contingent of hunters who fire their guns several times in a salute to us newcomers. "This is their way of welcoming you to Niafunke," Ali says. The town's residents have turned out to observe the goings on. One man in particular draws the attention of the visitors. He is tall and jet black, dressed

39

in a long and dirty robe. He screams in a high-pitched wail that seems to compete with the blasts of the shotguns. None of the locals are alarmed. People smile at him benevolently, as if he is the village idiot that everyone knows and cares for. This screaming is evidently normal behavior for this man, who otherwise appears unable or unwilling to talk. His eyes are ablaze.

The Hotel Campement is arranged around a central courtyard of green grass with narrow, concrete walkways that are bordered by brown sand. It is enclosed by mud brick and plaster walls, upon which the small, ubiquitous lizards known as margoya scurry back and forth, seeking shade from the hot sun. They resemble little crocodiles, their scaly bellies touching the ground. There is a bar, a small dining room and a kitchen where a silent chef from Mali's Dogon country will prepare whatever is on the menu. This is limited to fish, chicken, steak, fries, plantains, rice and salad. Sprite, Fanta, Castel, or Guinness are the drink selections. There are also a few tired old bottles of whiskey, gin and vodka. In a corner is a small one-man craft market. It makes up for its limited size by sheer variety and bright colors. There are many local textiles such as the bogolanfini (mudcloth) of the Bambara next to the large and colorful blankets of the Tuareg and the Peul (Fulani). There is silver jewelry, sandals, clothing and art.

Every night a table is set up with a television under a small tree. There is a concrete platform in the middle of the court yard. People come to share a drink, listen to music and watch satellite TV. Some nights it may be the news from the studios of ORTM (Radio Television Mali) in the capital city of Bamako, a talk show on Malian politics, or a big football match. Men drink beer and sodas, some smoke

cigarettes. Most women do not openly smoke, as it is as-
sociated with manliness, though some will smoke at home.
Often one can tell who are the prostitutes in a bar by observing which women are smoking while they drink. There
are none here, only couples or groups of men. Through the
wonders of the satellite dish people watch Brazillian soap
operas and reruns of Dallas, dubbed into French. When
there is an important football match, regular life is sus-
pended. Everyone is glued to the television, young and old.

I recall such a night sitting with Ali Farka, watching television under the stars. He is all royalty in a long
green embroidered boubou, clean black shoes and a white
cap. His bearing is regal, yet completely approachable. He
takes out his wallet to pay for the beers we have consumed,
brought from his bar in his hotel by his employee. I notice
a few credit cards, commonplace in the West but rare in
poorer countries such as Mali. This man supports and em-
ploys literally hundreds of people in one way or another,
yet lives in a tidy little mud-brick house on the banks of the
river. He is comfortable with all people, regardless of their
status or origin. He is a man of the people, one of the most
genuine souls you could ever meet. He has known wealth,
limited finances, hard work, leisure, disappointment and
triumph. He is full of stories, history, parables, the wisdom
of thousands of years of thought condensed into a simple
conversation. But it is more than just talking. Ali Farka
Toure does not merely talk to you. He holds court. People
are always coming to him for help, financial assistance, in-
vestment ideas and the like. He is wealthy and respected.
He loves to laugh and have a good time. His smile shines
like the sun. He attracts people effortlessly, by the sheer
weight of his personality. He respects all, but defers to no
one. He is his own man, at ease in the world. He drinks

his beer as if he is a patron of his own establishment while he smokes a few Dunhill cigarettes. There is nowhere in the world that he would rather be than in Niafunke. We check into our rooms at the hotel. They are sparse and clean. There is a nightstand, bed and separate shower and toilet. There is no shower curtain, just a drain in the floor, a sink, a towel rack and a mirror. A ceiling fan hangs from above and an air conditioner sits in the wall. I turn on the unit and it spits out a cloud of dust, the same dust that I could see floating in the atmosphere as we flew over the desert, 10,000 feet up in the sky. It is a fine haze that is everywhere. This is what makes every sunrise and sunset a work of art. Neither words on a page nor a photograph could ever do it justice. This is scenery to be stored away in the soul.

The next day we board a pinasse (large canoe) for the short trip across the ancient waterway where we will sit and talk and play music. On the way over Ali begins to play his njarka, the one-stringed fiddle with a snake rattle inside it that gives a touch of sweet distortion to its plaintive cries. He abruptly stops playing and gives me the small gourd instrument. I scratch out an njarka version of "Sittin' on Top of the World," an old blues song by the Mississippi Sheiks. Fish, water, music and the souls of Black folk come to mind. I see the Niger and think of the Mississippi. Rivers have been our lifeblood from time immemorial. They are the perennial super highways, the convergence of art, food, commerce, music, religion and culture. Africans have played music along rivers and upon rivers from the time of the ancient civilizations of the Nile, through the Congo, the Volta, the Gambia and the Joliba, the great river Niger. The red, gold and green of the Malian flag flies on a pole at the end of the pinasse. Someone has added the number seven in the center in bold script. It is the seventh month. We reach the other side of the river and descend from the pinasse on a long wooden plank. Here on the opposite shore there is a small village of Bozo fishermen and their families. The Bozo are renowned for their mystical connection to the river. It is said that when a person is feared drowned in the currents, a Bozo fisherman is called to 'talk with the river.' The Bozo can tell whether the person survived. If they died, the Bozo will know where the body can be found. They have been here for more than a thousand years.

When the Songhai first came to this land, they were here. They were here too when Ali's ancestors made their long march across the desert from Morocco. Now this is all Ali Farka's land, encompassing hundreds of acres on the bank opposite from Niafunke. As nobles of the Arma, his family has long held abundant land and cattle. His land holdings, like his herds of cattle, stretch into the desert horizon. He is a wealthy man, but he lives honestly and modestly. He loves to get his hands dirty and work hard. He gives generously to his family, friends and community. Introducing himself to a stranger, he would exclaim with a smile, "I am a farmer! Look at my hands!." Ali Farka Toure's large hands are strong and rough. His palms are calloused and the backs of his hands are blacker than obsidian. They are the hands of someone who is familiar with hard, manual labor under the heat of the desert sun. His music and spirit are tied to the soil, to the land of his forbearers. "Poverty and humility," Ali once told me, "that is the way."

We walk past a conglomeration of mud huts with red brick and zinc roofs. Small children are playing and some elders are sitting in the shade. Chickens and mules roam about as we walk into the sandy fields of Ali's nut and fruit orchards. He shows off the irrigation canals that he has dug to direct the muddy river water through his vast fields. After several minutes of walking atop generous furrows of dry earth, we reach a grove of trees and sit down. We take our guitars out of their cases and we begin to play. The blues is what we speak. A few children and some adults from the nearby Bozo village begin to gather around us to listen. We play and share verses in the key of E to the tune of "Catfish Blues" by Robert Petway. Muddy Waters made the song famous. We crossed muddy water to get here.

I close my eyes and can feel the Niger and the Mississippi river waters flowing together like music. Soon we put down our guitars and Ali leads a reasoning. In his Songhai-accented French he leads us through a thousand years of history, captivity, music and culture, weaving a tale that belongs to us both, Africa and her sons and daughters born in America. He knows about the Ma'afa (The Great Disaster) a.k.a. the Middle Passage and the enslavement of captive Africans. He is well aware that it was of no coincidence that African American blues and soul music reminded him of his own music. Seeing his love for all of that old blues and soul music is probably the most deeply touching moment I experience in Ali's presence. It is like a parent whose child was stolen from them years ago but they never stop looking for them, knowing they are out there somewhere. "I never forgot about you. You come from me."

44

"What I want to tell you is this: there are no 'Black Americans.' But there are Blacks in America. No, they don't exist at all. So, the Blacks left with their culture, which they had not lost, that is to say in their spirit. They have this knowledge, this familiarity. Their biography, ethnicity, legends, all these have been lost. But their music is African. Be it in the United States of America or in Mali, I observe that it is only cities and distances that separate us. But our souls, our spirits are the same. The same thing. There is no difference, not at all. Me, I have never felt it, and I even feel pity. Why? Because, after all, these are people that should be united.

My first time listening to John Lee Hooker, I heard his style and I said to myself, I don't understand. Where did they get this culture from? This is something that belongs to us! But, it is different, because he had to do something to survive. But, that right there, his style was not made neither for the whiskey, nor for the scotch, nor for the beer. [He smiles and laughs.] When a Black American comes to Africa, he does not need to feel like a foreigner. Because he has left home to come home. This is your territory. It is your umbilical cord. It is your inspiration. It is your knowledge within the wisdom. I know that there are ten million people who have come here. But I have never had so much joy like in these two days. So I am very grateful and I am obliged to thank you. What I wish is that as you have come in peace and prosperity, that you return in peace and prosperity to make a difference to those around you so that they can see the path. The path of peace and prosperity grounded in reality and mutual agreement. And here (he points to the earth we are sitting on) are the roots."

It is April, 2002. Ali has invited me to his modest and immaculate compound in Niafunke. His wife, a Bambara woman from southern Mali, greets me warmly. We remove our shoes and sit down inside. There are plenty of colorful Tuareg blankets and bogolanfini decorating the walls and the floors. There is little furniture inside the simple house. It is a small house for a great man. A large black and white photo of Ali sits above us. In it he is smiling and wearing a white suit and hat, the picture of vitality and health. He sits comfortably on the floor, barefoot, legs limberly crossed like a yogi. Ali's hands find his ngoni propped up against the wall. He begins to play as we talk about music, the blues, Africa, Black America. He has traveled widely and knows well the ways of the world beyond the Malian desert, but he would never think of living anywhere else but home. After a while he puts the instrument down and he turns on the television. The huge satellite dish perched on his roof beams in MTV. The sound is muted. A video featuring the Wu-Tang clan plays while images of hip hop and young, Black urban America flash across the screen. Old Dirty Bastard, the late rapper from Long Island, drops a rhyme as he flashes a grill of pure gold teeth. Ali looks mildly disgusted and asks me, "what is this shit?" I laugh, knowing that I couldn't offer a good explanation of hip-hop that would convince him otherwise. He dismisses it with a wave of his hand. Ali takes his music seriously. His music speaks of morality, history, struggle, love, African culture and social issues. For him, music is so much more than entertainment.

Soon the food is served. We eat riz casse (short grain brown rice), in tomato sauce with carrots, onions and cabbage. There is some meat offered which we soon find out is not beef, but rather porc-a-pic - porcupine. We are served cold, homemade yogurt for our dessert. It is sweet and salty at the same time. That evening I meet Boureima, also known as Vieux Farka, Ali's twenty year old son. He is quiet and polite. I am surprised to learn that he doesn't play music. Stouter and a little shorter than his father, he bears a strong resemblance to his Bambara mother. Five years later he will be crossing the globe, already a master at the guitar after only four years playing the instrument. Vieux will be the one who carries his father's musical legacy onwards to the future.

My room is a sauna. There is no breeze between these concrete walls, no air conditioning. The old ceiling fan does not work. So I sleep outside in the courtyard of this hotel on the banks of the river. Every day is hot, dry and dusty. Each morning I cough up a small measure of mud from breathing in the dust of the desert, but it is worth it to sleep under a vast quilt of stars. I am thankful for the breezes of the early morning, which blow fresh and cool off the river. It is the beginning of the rainy season, but dry as a bone here in the far western reaches of the Sahara. The next night I am with Ali, as usual. We are in his sister's home (one of several houses he owns in Mali), playing guitars and singing. It is early evening and we are taking advantage of the few hours of electricity that Niafunke's lone generator will give us before it shuts down for the evening. We are recording music for an album, 'Mississippi to Mali'. Two small microphones sit like stenographers, making a sonic chronicle of the proceedings. The walls are painted blue. I hear goats, chickens, and donkeys outside. Children play. Muddy water flows. Crickets chirp. It is as if all creation collaborates with us in making the music. Accompanying us are some friends and fellow musicians. Among them is the quietly superb guitarist, Ali Magassa,

47

and the solid and tireless percussionist, Souleyman Kane. Soon the Niger swallows up the sun and it turns pitch black outside. Insects are drawn to the light bulbs that are illuminating our session. They begin to swarm. We keep playing until the generator is turned off and the lights go out. I walk back to the hotel, wading through the darkness, thick and black like the river. I lie down to sleep, tucked away under a nightly sheet of desert starlight. It seems that every night is exactly like this one, with my mind afloat in a sea of desert music. Who can imagine that eleven years from now, all music will be banned in Niafunke?

THE SLEEPING GIANT

"When you follow in the path of your father, you learn to walk like him."

- Ashanti proverb

*I*t is Wednesday, Dec. 21, 2011. I have come to Bamako with my videographer to visit Boureima "Vieux" Farka Toure at the family house in the Lafiabougou neighborhood. Riding in the taxi on the way to the house we see young men and boys walk alongside donkeys carrying heavy loads while beggars young and old sit with outstretched hands for their daily bread. Children are everywhere, walking in groups or playing in doorways by the side of the busy road. A young mother bathes her baby in a large plastic tub next to the front door of their compound. The sandstone cliffs that border this western quarter of town are bathed in the warm December sun of the afternoon. Take away the buildings and the people and it looks like a scene from somewhere in Arizona or New Mexico, with the arid landscape and flat mesas. It is the dry season and the dust is everywhere. It mixes with the smells of cooking from near and distant courtyards and the heavy exhaust from cars, mopeds and trucks which navigate the dirt side streets and paved thoroughfares. I pay the taxi driver the

1,500 CFA fare and send him on his way. He drives away slowly, maneuvering around the potholes and bumps in the dirt road. Sitting outside the house along a white exterior wall are a few men of various ages. Three among the group appear to be in their early twenties, while another man with a stocky build and chocolate skin tone seems to be a few years older. There is one elder among them, a fit, kind-looking man with an immaculate bald head and a jet black complexion. His youthful, healthy appearance belies the deep wisdom of his eyes. Greetings are exchanged as we pass them to enter the compound.

The two-story house is undergoing a heavy renovation and there is sand and cinder blocks near the entrance. The courtyard is full of people, young men and women who are cousins or friends of the family. The men are busy coming and going, helping out with chores around the large compound. A large mango tree is the focal point of the yard. Under its green leaves the young women are preparing the day's meal, fanning coals on an outdoor stove. Some young men smoke cigarettes, listen to music on their cellphones, or just talk. Vieux sits in a lawn chair in the shade of the tree, smoking Dunhill cigarettes, laughing and talking. He pauses once in a while to speak to a younger cousin or to give some money with instructions to buy this or that for the house. The language is Songhai, with an occasional French word thrown in. Being here feels like an outpost of northern Mali in the middle of Bamako. Vieux stands up and leads us to a tidy, simply decorated living room with large sofas covered in maroon-colored leather. The upholstered furniture looks brand new against the white walls. On the wall are pictures of Vieux and his wife Ami from their wedding in the northern city of Gao, her hometown. There is a small framed picture of Ali Farka and Toumani

Diabate, smiling warmly like old friends. Two young men are busy repairing the broken air conditioning unit on the wall next to the sofa. A stereo sits in a corner across from the sofa where we are seated. Next to it is another black and white photograph of his father looking calmly, intently into the camera. He is youthful and vibrant. Ali bought this house in nineteen eighty-four. He has been gone for six years now.

We have a seat inside and wait for Vieux. He lingers in the courtyard speaking with several of the young men assembled under the mango tree. A little while later some fresh fish is brought into the courtyard and the young women begin to cook it for us while the others in the courtyard eat rice and fish. I drink green tea with mint while we wait. Soon Vieux's younger brother Hasay comes in to say hello. The two brothers strike slightly different figures in the dim light of the living room. Vieux's face and stocky frame favor their Bambara mother while Hasay's thin frame and features are strikingly similar to their father. The brothers give a brief tour of the house, talking about the renovations in progress. The bedrooms are finished and furnished, though there is still work that needs to be done in the bathrooms. Everything is tiled and color coordinated. There is a large upstairs living room with a huge flat screen television mounted on a wall of stone masonry. Soon we sit down to eat fried fish -- Capitaine (Nile perch) -- with rice and tomato sauce.

After the meal is finished Vieux begins to talk about his father. He was not raised by Ali, but by his uncle, Ali's younger brother who lived near Mopti, a small city at the intersection of the Niger and Bani rivers, eight hours by road from the capital. Vieux recalls that his father would visit sometimes during breaks from his heavy touring schedule. Over the years he spent long periods of time away from his father. This is not uncommon in Africa where uncles and aunts have the same status as parents and cousins are equal to siblings. As a child, Vieux was interested in joining the army, but changed his mind after he saw what war was like. "I hate war," he says. Then his ambitions turned to music. When he told Ali about his new ambition, his father didn't approve. Ali Farka knew the crooked nature of the music business, the problems with management and not getting paid well. "Sometimes he would earn five or ten thousand (CFA) and the manager would take ten or fifteen percent. He didn't like that." The difference between his experience and that of his son is that Vieux had been to school and was literate in French. Ali was not. A few times in the past he had fallen victim to the schemes of European promoters and agents who knew that he could not read English or French and presented him with unfair contracts. "You know that's not like him. He have something...he just sign. He don't know what's happening."

It is worth noting here that written contracts are largely a convention of the western world, where the value of a man's word is small. In traditional Africa, one's word is bond. A man's word was the contract. Ali acted in accordance with his culture and the upbringing of his times when he took the Europeans at their word. Vieux is of a different generation. "When you send me something, I look at it. I read everything and I say, 'I don't like this, I don't like that.' If you send me a contract in English I say, 'No, no, no! French! So I have to see everything." Children's laughter floats through the window from next door as Vieux sits on his couch in the living room. He is glad to see that people are still interested in his father. "Where we are from we say that there are those who are finished, there are people who are dead, and there are those who just went to lay down. Those who are finished are they who have left nothing of themselves. No children, no wife...they have nothing! The people don't even know them. They are finished now. There are those who are dead but they do have a family, children, a house. But those who went to sleep, are those who have done a lot in their life and their name will always be known among the people. That's the people who went away to sleep. They are always there." He smiles. Surely his father is one of those whom he speaks about, a sleeping giant. "Every person who has something that they have bought...things in their house...the name is always there. My father would say that there are people who talk about heaven and hell. He thought all of that is bullshit. All of that is here." Vieux points to the ground beneath our feet. "Everything happens here. You see everything in this life before you go." Vieux is calm, confident and self-assured. He has inherited his father's nobility in more ways than one. All of these qualities come out in his music.

"Nobles don't play music. Me, I'm not a griot [djeli]. I don't play griot music. I don't even know how to do it." He says that he makes music to make people happy, to awaken their conscience, to educate them. His music sprang from the root that his father established. It is the same music; when you hear the father you also hear the son. "It is like when you have something in a bag and you take it out and put in next to the bag. It's the same thing. When you have a pot of water and you fill a glass from it, it's still the same water." Vieux began playing music slowly, over a period a several years. "It happened all at once but also slowly. There are a lot of people who play music and there are many who are very good at it. But it is also important to know that music is a question of luck. I think that is true. There are a lot of people who started before me." In 1994 he began playing the djembe. As he puts it, in 2001 he said to himself, "This is good. I will try and play the guitar a little bit." He started to progress quickly after this. That same year, when he started telling others that he was playing the guitar, they said, "You are crazy." He enrolled in the Ecole National de Beaux Arts (National School of the Arts), a legendary forming ground for many of the top artists of Mali. There is rigorous instruction in every field, from music and dance to the visual arts as well as television and radio broadcasting. Though his father was at first against the idea of Vieux making a career in music, he eventually gave him his blessing. Ali was getting weaker from fighting the cancer that was ravaging his bones. He was in his last days and he knew it.

In 2004 and 2005 his father took Vieux under his wing, teaching him the guitar style that made him famous. "That was worth ten years of apprenticeship, the few months that I studied with him." He recorded in 2005 and the album came out in 2006. Some might say that Vieux knew at the time that he would take his father's place because of Ali's terminal illness. But it wasn't like that. After all, who can replace Ali Farka? He was one of a kind. "I don't know how (he started playing with his father)...it was the work of God. It just happened." Vieux's humility and gratitude towards his father is obvious. The photos hanging on the wall are so clear that Ali's face seems to jump out of their frames in approval. He says that to really know about his father, I should speak with Oumar Toure. As if on cue, Oumar and his nephew Samba walk in from the courtyard through sliding glass doors. They come over to where we are sitting and share a handshake and a smile with Vieux. This is family. I see he is the same bald-headed elder with the kind, wise face that I observed sitting outside. Samba is the stocky, middle aged man I saw at the entrance with him. They both sit down and listen attentively as Vieux speaks about the long history of Ali and Oumar. Where Ali Farka Toure was gregarious and vigorous with a booming voice, Oumar is soft-spoken, calm. He says that Vieux is just like Ali, taking care of many people at once, both friends and family. It is dark now, but youth of various ages are still in the courtyard, coming and going according to the chores at hand. It is time to leave, so Vieux calls us a taxi and we say goodbye. On the way back to the hotel I can hear Vieux's guitar mixing with his father's unmistakable drone in the back of my mind. The guitar lines snake together and become inseparable, like sands swirling in a desert storm.

BROTHER'S KEEPER

"There is no better mirror than an old friend."
- Cape Verdian proverb

*B*amako, 1965. It is five years since Mali has gained its independence from France. The colonizers have done their best to mis-educate the population about their true history, giving them school books which tell them only about French history and nothing of their own. Those children whose hard-working parents are able to send them to school are force-fed historical lies. Text books tell them about "our ancestors, the Gauls" while the true history of the nation as told by the djeli is officially ignored. Knowledge is power and the control of knowledge by the oppressor ensures that the exploitation of the oppressed will continue. Culture is the glue that holds a nation together. It is also the path of liberation from a colonial mentality. This new generation of Malians, led by President Modibo Keita, is committed to change. They have been doing the hard work of nation-building. La Semaine National de la Jeunesse (National Youth Week) is crucial to achieve this goal, mobilizing the youth towards the unity that must prevail if this new multi-ethnic republic is to succeed. The festival is modeled after the Quinzaine de la Jeunesse, (Fif-

56

teen Days of Youth) established by President Sekou Toure in neighboring Guinea, which was also once a part of ancient Mali. Youth from each of the six regions in Mali have come to Bamako to competitively showcase their athletic abilities and the artistic traditions of the different regions. There are actors, playwrights, musicians and athletes, all here to inspire and represent the future of the new nation. Among them are a young Ali Farka Toure and his soon-to-be lifelong friend and confidant, Oumar Toure. There is excitement in the air, the future is bright and a new Africa is on the move.

The week begins with a large gathering of the public, government officials and the young participants at the stadium in Bamako. Various government ministers are assembled to inaugurate the upcoming event and to talk about its importance. It is summertime, the rainy season. Heavy, black clouds have been gathering and churning in the skies all afternoon. After one of the ministers gives a lengthy speech, the pregnant clouds release their waters and there is a sudden downpour. Everyone is running around, seeking shelter from the rain. Young Oumar Toure is among them. He has come to Bamako with other youths from his area representing the delegation from Gao, an ancient city in the deserts of northern Mali near the border with Niger, though he comes from Dire, a small town in the Timbuktu region. Both the delegations of Gao and Mopti are being housed in Bamako's Technical High School. Each group wears distinctive clothes to show where they have come from. The Gao delegation is dressed in all white, while those from Mopti are wearing bogolanfini. When Oumar comes inside to seek shelter from the storm, he finds himself surrounded by the Mopti delegation. He stands out in his white clothes and right away some rough youths from Mopti yell at him to get out. Oumar tells them, "I'm leaving." Just as he is heading for the door one of the youths pushes him and he falls right on to a tall, dignified young man carrying an acoustic guitar. They both fall to the ground and the guitar is broken. But instead of getting angry at Oumar, the tall stranger announces to everyone in a loud voice that Oumar is not leaving. Somebody yells, "But he is not from Mopti!" They have been strangers up until now, but the young man in bogolanfini says, "No, he is my brother." Some of the greatest meetings often happen by accident, and so it was that Oumar Toure literally fell upon Ali Farka Toure on a rainy evening in Bamako. One might say it was an accident that was meant to be. Before their story is finished these two young Malians will travel the world together, and one of them will become an international star and the other his brother's keeper. But tonight they are just two talented young men who are full of dreams about their future in a Mali free from French rule. Ali Farka Toure will become a fixture of the Semaine de la Jeunesse, playing the annual festival for several years after his debut. Everyone is taken by the young guitar master from Niafunke. Farka always comes in first. Eventually the organizers withdraw him from the competition and an ngoni player and an njarka player are brought in to replace him. He has outgrown the festival. Farka is already a star at home, though he is not yet known outside of Mali.

That evening the youths are given tickets by the event organizers to attend several concerts being held in the city. Tonight the musicians from Mopti are supposed to play. The young men and women perform all dressed in the traditional bogolanfini. They are strong, black, noble, and conscious of their moment in time. Many of them are

Peul or Fulani, as this city on the Niger is traditionally their dominion. They sing in traditional languages; Songhai, Peul, Tamasheck, Bambara. Ali sings in his native Songhai, the language of the nation that became a mighty empire and ruled Mali for centuries. Oumar is Songhai too. They and all the other youths are the future of the new nation. Africa is breaking the chains of colonialism and traditional culture is the way. Everyone is dressed crisp and clean, regal, colorful and dignified. Some of the men are wearing western clothing, but most of the people are in traditional attire: long boubous, dresses made of the finest fabrics in every hue and color, elegant headwraps, finely worked leather sandals and shoes, gold and silver jewelry. Clothes are so fresh and starched-stiff that they rustle like sheets of paper. There is a faint smell of frankincense in the air.

Oumar is in the audience, and as soon as he sees Ali, he says to his friend, "Ahh! That's who saved me today." He doesn't see Ali anymore that week, but he remembers his new friend, the tall, noble guitar master from Niafunke. Later that same year, Niafunke and Dire are made sister villages. Ali has come to Dire with an orchestra and some football players to entertain the residents of Dire. Oumar, a guitarist and bassist, is chosen to accompany Ali Farka. They play a song by James Brown, an artist who perhaps more than any other Black American has influenced generations of Africans. After they are finished playing, Oumar introduces himself to Ali: "Do you remember when you saved me in Bamako?" Ali smiles and says, "Yes, I remember!" Before he leaves Dire for the long trip back to Niafunke, he says to a friend, "Take care of him. He is my brother." After this experience, Oumar begins to listen to Ali's music a lot, trying to emulate his sound on the

59

guitar whenever he can. Ali's music is steadily becoming more popular and the national radio plays it all the time. His music is also becoming well-known in Niger and other neighboring countries. Ali is becoming increasingly well-known, first in Mali and later across the entire continent. After a while, the word gets around to Ali that there is a young man in Dire who plays just like him. Their friendship grows. Whenever Ali comes to Dire to play he stays with Oumar and his family. He lends Oumar a guitar to accompany him. By this time Oumar knows all of Ali's music and falls right in, playing with him easily. As the years go by, Ali visits Oumar whenever he is passing through Dire. Though they are not related by blood, the two Toures become like the closest of brothers.

It is 1980. Oumar has relocated to Ivory Coast to teach in a sewing school (he is a trained tailor). Abidjan is a tropical and bustling modern metropolis, world away from the arid expanses of northern Mali. Word reaches him that Ali has come to town to play a concert. On a particular Saturday Oumar goes to see Ali. He is playing two concerts and a wedding and asks his old friend to accompany him. After they finish playing he tells Oumar, "My brother, you need to return home, because here in Ivory Coast is not good." Looking back on that time thirty-one years ago Oumar says, "So right away I thought of a lie to tell my boss that I have to return to my country because my father had passed away. If I didn't do that, he would not have let me go." His nephew Samba blurts out with a smile and a chuckle: "But then he found out that his father had been dead a long time!" Oumar smiles along with him. He continues, "Yes, he had actually died. So it wasn't a lie. But when I told them, all the students there cried! I regretted the lie and thought to myself, 'Why did I say that?

I'm not going to leave anymore.' I was obliged to make up something...all my friends there, they were crying!" Oumar is talking about death, but now everyone in the room is laughing. We are laughing at our love for life, despite all of its tears, calamity and unforeseen tragedies.

Oumar leaves his job teaching sewing in Abidjan and returns to Dire. A few months after Oumar returns home, Ali comes to town to play a concert at the invitation of some Italians who work at a hospital. Oumar plays with him. Ali has come with an English journalist, Andy Kershaw.. They spend two days together, talking. Afterwards, Ali says, "I don't know if I will have a lot of work here. There are contracts in Europe and we can go there together." Oumar tells him, "Yes, I would like that, but I have to travel. I will let you know when I get back and we can go together." In the meantime, Oumar visits his elder brother who lives in Burkina Faso. They have worked together many times in the past and he has done a lot to help Oumar. He mentions this new opportunity with Ali Farka to his brother, who encourages him to accept the offer. "I would like to see Europe and America," Oumar tells his brother. His eyes sparkle in the dimly lit room as he remembers the first time. When he returns from Burkina Faso he calls Ali and says simply, "Ok, I'm here." In no time at all he is in Bamako signing papers to get his passport. The dream of traveling to Europe and America is becoming a reality. "So that's how we started working together, just the two of us. I played the congas, the calabash, sometimes the guitar." It is 1989 and Ali Farka Toure's career is really about to take off. The duo tours often in Switzerland, England and other parts of Europe. As is so often the case with new artists who are eager to work, they are taken advantage of. The promoter, a European woman with whom Ali has signed a contract, is paying them only 75,000 CFA ($150.00) per show. This amount is for them both to split; the promoter pays Ali and Ali pays Oumar. These are lean times. There is no way they can support their families back home on this, but they do what they have to do, hoping something better will come along. It soon does. Ali knows another European woman who is in the music industry. When she sees what is going on with the promoter, she says, "Ali you are totally crazy. How can she take millions off of your back and afterwards give you whatever?" Upon hearing this, Ali immediately breaks the contract. It is said that when one door closes, another door opens. It isn't long before he receives a call from a Frenchman named Olivier, with whom he was able to earn a little more. By this time, Ali has joined forces with a producer named Nick Gold. He owns World Circuit, a record company based in the U.K. He suggests that Ali break the contract and sign with a man in London named David Flauvert who can pay Ali better. Ali breaks the second contract and soon he and Oumar find their way to London.

Eventually Ali makes contacts in the U.S. and hires a manager, an American woman named Deborah. He and Oumar continue to travel and play music together. One day Ali suggests to Nick that he borrow enough money to start a booking agency. Ali is not just a musician, but a sharp businessman as well. "We need to start a booking agency so that we can work!" Nick asks his father, who lends them the money to start the agency. "So it was like that up until nineteen ninety-five when we got the Grammy. We made the cassette with Ry Cooder and Clarence Gatemouth Brown who is dead now. He plays the violin and is very good on the guitar, with the big hat...very skinny!" Soon they are doing promotion in Africa, Europe and America. They are bringing some younger players ("enfants") on the road with them now. But no one can replace Oumar. "Ali really liked me a lot, I don't know why. He liked me, he trusted in me, he loved my work more than anyone. Ali and me...I'm his friend, I'm his little brother, I'm his employee. He always accepted me. He didn't hide anything from me. He told me everything, all his secrets. On the road I have even slept in the same bed with him. I'm the only one who does that. We did everything together." Ali Farka struggled through meager times to reach the heights of greatness and Oumar was with him every step of the way.

"So during the first edition (2001) of Essakane, the Festival in the Desert, I came out of the tent with him. I remember he had a beer. There was a Frenchwoman there, a certain Catherine. We went over to the dunes and sat down. There was somebody who came asking Ali if he would participate in a program that they were putting together for the Folklife Festival [in Washington, D.C.]. So he couldn't refuse. Every time anything developed in Africa, at home, he would go do it, but he didn't want to go chasing money in Europe or America anymore." Sitting with them is a journalist who asks Ali if he would do the festival. He looks at Oumar, "If my brother Oumar accepts." Oumar says, "No problem. We will go." He gives the names of five or six people who will be accompanying Ali. Ali's appearance at the Folklife festival is still two years and a world away. Catherine and the journalist finish their conversation with Ali and Oumar and walk away. They sit and talk, taking in the cool nighttime breeze. The dunes of Essakane dwarf the festival grounds and absorb the sublime sounds of Malian music while the crowd drinks it all in like cool water from a desert oasis. The cloudless night sky makes the stars seem close enough to touch. The ancient strains of traditional Malian music, the singing, strings and drums, ricochet off the dunes. The whole scene is tranquil, serene. Ali looks at Oumar with a serious look on his face and says, "My brother, I feel I have some sort of illness." He points to the side of his abdomen. His expression tells Oumar that he is in pain. As he looks back on that night nearly ten years ago, Oumar says, "This started to scare me. After a few months his condition began to get worse. I think he just said it like that....he told me that he was feeling that something's not right. I am his confidante. After that, we went to Morocco. There, he let me know that he had a problem with his prostate. I told him, 'You need to stop everything today and go to Paris. Take care of it immediately.' He was the type who was very...[searches for a word]...he didn't accept it. He had too much confidence in himself." Oumar sees the urgency of the situation, but his old friend does not fully accept his condition. Now it has become much worse. Sitting on a chair in Vieux's house in Bamako, he remembers the pain of watching his old friend become ill. He sucks his teeth and shakes his head. If only Ali had listened and sought early treatment, perhaps he would still be alive today....

"He told me to get ready, that we are going to Burkina Faso. Actually I was the one who had made this contract. I brought it, because Ali said that he did not want to go. So when they telephoned Ali when the date had arrived, Ali had told me to go." Oumar hesitates, knowing Ali's deteriorating health. Up until now they have never worked without the other. Without asking Ali, he declines the invitation. "I told them I can't go and they should ask Ali. So Ali called me and said, 'Why did you say that?

Come on, you all go, even if I don't go. You need to go do it, it's an engagement.' We [Ali and Oumar] went to Burkina Faso together to the Jazz Festival there. There's a brother there who was asking to see Ali. I said no problem. He and I went to see Ali at the hotel so that Ali could give the ok for the contract. It ended up that Ali could not go, so we went, me, Vieux...it was five of us so we went and did it, without Ali. He told us to go and do it. Ali was very happy when we returned because the amount of money he could charge for appearances in Africa was three million CFA [approx.. $6000.00] and here in Mali it was one million CFA [approx. $2,000.00]. When I came I brought the money and left it with him and he cried. He told me that it's ok, even if he were to die today there are younger ones coming up behind him who can continue on the path."

In the following months, there is an improvement in Ali's health and he resumes touring. He even begins to walk again. They fly to Conakry and tour Guinea, Mali's verdant and fertile sister nation with which it shares a border. Soon afterwards, Ali goes to the hospital in Paris for a routine treatment. Then it's back on the road to play concerts in Brussels and Italy before returning to France. The cancer strikes again when they are in Nice. Ali rapidly falls very ill and is completely immobilized. He lapses into a deep coma. The other players of the group return home to Mali but Oumar remains in France with his old friend. They stay in Nice for two days, Oumar takes care of his friend and figures out what can be done. With the help of Deborah (Ali's manager) and others, Oumar travels with Ali to visit the doctor in Paris. However when they finally reach the doctor, he says that he cannot receive Ali because he had asked him to schedule an appointment four months ago and Ali didn't come. The doctor doesn't seem to realize or care that the severity of Ali's illness at the time made him unable to keep the appointment. The doctor says coldly that Ali has to wait three more days because he had a lot of patients and Ali did not keep the original appointment. Only outside of Africa would someone of Ali's stature be subjected to such treatment when he was clearly in need of help. This doctor seems to want to punish Ali Farka for not following his instructions. Once an African, always an African, for better or for worse. African nobility, talent, status, generosity and humility don't seem to count here in Europe.

"So there was a Frenchwoman who was taking care of things with Ali's sickness and she negotiated with the doctor to have Ali come the next day at ten o'clock. So the next day at ten o'clock they came with the ambulance and we all went to the doctor. So when we came, the doctor took him in the back and we were in the waiting room. A woman came out after the doctor had come and we asked, 'Is it going to be alright?' She said, 'Yes...he was given a treatment that was a bit difficult and he might die. But if it is successful then it will be ok.' Her words give no comfort. The gravity of the situation is settling in. "Afterwards, the doctor said that we should not count on Ali getting better. He had terminal cancer and it had already entered the blood and the bones. The doctor said it is very serious and that he couldn't live more than four or five months. When he said that, Ali was getting up to leave. He was behind the doctor, but the doctor didn't know he was there. He said it just like that. Ali himself did not want me to hear that. He was walking like this [demonstrates difficulty walking]. Ali was going out and the door was open and as he was getting up the doctor said that he wouldn't live more than four or five months. When he said that, I was very sad. I didn't

66

cry and Ali didn't cry either." Even though they know he is very sick, everyone is surprised by this. This is Ali Farka, the man whose middle name means donkey, who has always supported so many people with his generosity. It is hard to imagine him being laid low by cancer, immobile, helpless. "So when we got in the car, I was here and he was there, just like how he was when he was in the ambulance [Oumar demonstrates Ali reclining in the chair]. I saw that he had some [tissue] paper. He did like this [wipes his eyes]...he was crying. The shock of the doctor's sudden pronouncement is almost too much to bear. This is the first time Oumar realizes how sick Farka really is. He is visibly shaken, but he tries to comfort Oumar. "My brother, don't get discouraged. There are illnesses here that the doctor can't do anything with. We will go to Mali, to the Dogon Country and take care of this." Oumar knows Ali is just saying this to make his old friend feel better. They return to the Hotel Manet, the only hotel they have stayed at in Paris for the past twenty years. They are well known here.

Ali could have easily afforded a fancier, more expensive hotel, but he prefers this unassuming two-star establishment tucked along on a narrow side street near the Place d'Italie. Whenever they come they are welcomed like family. They are met by a large gathering of well-wishers from Africa, the United States, and Europe. Farka is very happy to see everyone who has come to the hotel to show their support for him. It is afternoon and Ali is hungry. He has not eaten since before leaving for the hospital. Soon the food is brought out and everyone sits down to share a meal together. There are smiles and laughter all around. Ali quietly tells Oumar that the area on his abdomen where the doctor had performed the treatment is feeling bad. Oumar says, "Let's go to the room." Ali is very frail and unable to walk, so Oumar carries him to the elevator and takes him to his room on the seventh floor. When they reach the room, Oumar places him in a recliner and sits down on a sofa. Suddenly Ali begins to cry. Oumar has never heard him cry like this. Ali exclaims, "Is this how I am going to die?" Oumar is startled to see his friend who was once strong and vibrant, now dependent and afraid. After some time, Ali falls asleep and Oumar calls the doctor to say that it wasn't going well. The doctor comes to the hotel and stays the rest of the day until eleven o'clock in the evening. By now all of the assembled well-wishers have all gone to bed. Now it is just Ali and Oumar at the hotel. Oumar looks back on that day five years ago: "I was the only one left with him. I am his brother. Me, I thought he was going to die. Everyone was thinking this." After about thirty minutes Ali began to move a little bit. Oumar is tired and falls asleep in his room across the hall from Ali's room. He is so tired that he doesn't even take his shoes off.

At about three in the morning, Oumar's telephone rings. He wonders to himself, "Who can this be, calling me like this?" Oumar answers. It is Ali. He says, "Toure!" Oumar says, "Ali!" and races out of the room to see what is the matter with his friend. Oumar sees that Ali has awakened during the night. He has propped himself up in bed. Oumar stops at the door and tentatively calls Farka's name. Ali replies, "Yes." Oumar says, "How is it going?" Ali says, "It is going very well." Ali says it like he was sure that he was doing better. There is a strength in his voice that Oumar has not heard for some time. Ali says that he is hungry, so right away Oumar goes downstairs to the hotel kitchen, puts some food together and brings it up. "We have everything there: chicken, vegetables, fruit...here it's all for us since we have been coming here for twenty years together." To Oumar's surprise, Ali eats everything, the chicken, the vegetables and three full bowls of yogurt! It seems like Farka is finding his strength again. Oumar says to himself, "I don't believe it! Is this a dream or is this reality?" After Ali eats, Oumar can see that his old friend needs to rest. He tells him that he will go back to his room across the hall. Ali says, "No, let's make tea." Oumar makes strong mint tea, just like they do at home in Mali. He boils the water, and adds the dry, green tea. It is jet black and looks like gunpowder. When the tea leaves have boiled long enough, he adds fresh mint and a generous portion of sugar. Tea in Mali is more than a simple hot drink.

When he leaves, Ali is sleeping soundly in his bed. Oumar wakes up around seven o'clock, bathes and goes downstairs to the hotel restaurant. He finds that the same well-wishers and friends from the day before are all waiting in the restaurant. There is a somber feeling in the air. They all know how ill Ali is and they are thinking that he has died during the night. When Oumar appears, everyone rises suddenly from where they are sitting, all with worried looks on their faces. Oumar says simply, "It's okay. It's okay." He tells them about all the food Ali had eaten earlier that morning, the chicken, the yogurt and the tea. They are all amazed. "Wow!" The room erupts in laughter, happiness, dancing. Oumar eats breakfast with the group and then retreats upstairs to look in on Ali. "I'm the only one who can go in his room. I opened the door very quietly. I saw that he was in the bathroom. I said, 'Everybody is waiting.' He said okay, he can go out. He just had to change his boubou [shirt]." Oumar brings the boubou and Ali puts it on with the matching pants. They take the elevator downstairs and when they come out they hear some music playing on the television. Now, in front of everyone, Ali starts to dance. He is beaming. Pure joy fills the room like rays of sunlight. All the people assembled there that day – Africans, Europeans, Americans – are witnessing a miracle. Death has lost this battle, for now. It is time to celebrate.

SEGU BY BUS

"All journeys have secret destinations of which the traveler is unaware."

- Martin Buber

We are glad to leave Bamako, Mali's bustling and sprawling capital city of two million souls. The exhaust of the cars and trucks mixed with the omnipresent dust is almost unbearable. We are on our way to Segu, a tranquil town famous for its fabrics and traditional art. Both are situated on the banks of the Joliba, the heart and ancient highway of this landlocked West African nation. Today our highway is on land. We will take it north, riding a public coach as it follows the river to Segu. We are told that the trip will take three or four hours at the most. However, in Africa, time is often relative to the conditions at hand. A traveler might have at first imagined a breezy few hours' evening drive through the dry Sahel. Now it has turned into a hot and rainy test of mental and physical endurance on a crowded bus of the late 1970's vintage variety. There are several stops: picking up more passengers, paying bribes to local police at checkpoints and stopping for purchases of food and drink with the requisite cigarette and bathroom breaks. Sometimes we stop for what seems to be

71

no reason at all. Each time a stop is made, the driver cuts off the engine to save fuel while more passengers climb aboard. Soon frustration, anger, heat and claustrophobia take hold of several people until it almost reaches a boiling point. "Mais c'est quoi chauffeur?!!" ("Driver what is going on?!!") exclaims a full-figured Bambara woman, brown like a chocolate drop with her head tied up in indigo fabric. Everyone is sweating in the musty air of the crowded bus. Eventually the engine starts up, and we are on our way again, this time with the air-conditioner blowing cool air. Everyone is thankful.

At each stop there are small roadside kitchens with zinc roofing on top of a rough wood frame to make a shelter for tables and a few chairs. One thin, olive-skinned Tuareg man in a western, collared shirt and well-ironed slacks descends from the bus to relieve himself and take in the scene. His traveling companion is an older Tuareg man in traditional attire. The thin man brushes off the many vendors and lights a cigarette. There are open fires to cook food. Vendors here sell meat, peanuts, Coke, Sprite, water and brightly colored sodas in small plastic bottles. There is also a spicy, home-made ginger drink, and bissap, a dark red, sweet drink made from hibiscus. These refreshments are sold both in bottles and small plastic bags that the customer must puncture to suck out the cool juice. Chickens, goats, oranges, and a vast selection of local fruits and vegetables dominate the scene. Some women and girls are selling beans and rice with sweet coffee. People, mostly women and young girls, walk on the side of the highway or sit at roadside stalls selling various food and myriad supplies. Young men are doing the hard work of taking orders and hauling merchandise. The woman is the Queen of the market in Africa. I can feel the countless generations of prosperous Africans who through the millennia mastered the art of the sell. These are the convenience stores of the community. Many people are walking, some with bags, while others balance steep loads upon the crowns of their heads. They glide along. Others ride bicycles or speed along on scooters, the favored transport in this once mighty empire. Everybody is working. Everything is in motion, from early morning into the latest night. The bus driver sounds the horn and the passengers all climb onboard. We are on our way again. Night falls, and the vast expanses of seemingly empty Sahel and dry brush turn to black. The only light comes from the headlights of passing vehicles or the occasional lightning flash from the seasonal thunderstorm which is now pelting our sometimes air-conditioned bus with heavy rains. Departing Bamako, the driver had jammed the bus with as many passengers as he could fit: luggage, hefty canisters of palm oil, cords of fire wood, large bags of food and even larger market sacs at whose contents one could only guess. All of this is packed in the overhead storage, or when space runs out, simply placed on the floor and in the aisle. We all have to climb over this colorful conglomeration to reach our seats. No one complains.

The thunderstorm still rages outside with no sign of stopping. Blue lightning strikes flash like a strobe, illuminating the barren landscape for a few seconds before fading quickly to black. At times both sides of the road are flanked by expanses of shallow water. I start to wonder if the road ahead will be flooded out at places. Malian popular music and American hip-hop and R&B play, while passengers chat in Bambara, Pulaar, Tomashek, Songhai and French on their cell phones. Soon the roof springs a leak, clear water dripping down slowly on a young, dark-skinned woman with straightened hair sitting across the aisle from

73

me. Another leak appears above my seat. Buses, gros camions (large trucks), 4x4 vehicles, and a few small cars make their way through the storm, immediately engulfed by the darkness as soon as they pass our overloaded coach. The night swallows up every lighting strike like a black hole devours a star.

By the time we reach Segu, the long road has taken its toll on everyone. Passengers disembark from the bus, seeming to explode out of the narrow entrance. Groups of youths working as porters descend upon the mass of luggage, directing travelers towards taxis or clandestine drivers. The autogare (bus station) is nothing more than a cluster of mud buildings with zinc or thatched roofs situated on the main road a couple of kilometers away from the town center. Some more solidly constructed buildings stand out with their white walls and heavy metal doors. Being very close to the river, insects swarm near every light bulb shining in the darkness. A few small stores sell various staple items such as bottled water, green tea, sugar, canned milk, tissues, batteries, and other goods under the white light of florescent bulbs. Some of these spaces are no more than recycled shipping containers. I had imagined this area would be bustling with commerce and activity in the daylight hours. Now it is nearly deserted, with a few stray dogs and people who look like they are used to staying up late. Once we find our taxi and the luggage is loaded inside, we find that this dilapidated, old white Renault will not start. Loathe to lose his new customers, the driver quickly finds some people to help push the car until it starts. One of the helpers seems quite amused, laughing and light-heartedly mocking the driver as he and a few others push. The driver clearly doesn't think any of this is funny. He scowls and grumbles under his breath as he tries to get the car to

74

start. I can see that he is not a regular taxi driver, but a moonlighter who is barely getting by. Finally the engine comes alive and we are moving. We make our way through dimly lit streets into the center of town and to our hotel on the banks of the great river. Hardly a soul walks the streets. Everyone is shuttered up at home, asleep.

The hotel is called L'Auberge. Owned by two Lebanese brothers, it hosts mainly expatriates, well-to-do Malians, government officials, Peace Corps volunteers and European tourists. The latter are often dressed backpacker style, with dingy grey and brown colors, camouflage, bandanas, hiking boots and safari hats. Their choice of clothing shows what they think of Africa: an untamed wilderness requiring specialized equipment found at the camping store. All the while, even the some of the poorest Malians dress cleanly with vivid colors and sharp lines, looking curiously at the rich westerners who are very conspicuous in their grungy Rambo-camouflage chic. They look foolish. There is a pool, and the restaurant serves a melange of local and western oriented cuisine: pommes frites, (fries), capitaine, (aka Nile perch), omelets, and the usual hamburger and chicken dishes. Aloko (fried plantains) is a staple. The avocados are the best in the world. Americans are always easy to spot, as they are the only patrons asking for ketchup and plenty of ice. Both are relatively scarce commodities here in Mali's third largest city.

Segu was once a powerful kingdom, waging intermittent wars with neighboring states such as the kingdom of Kaarta to add to its expanding realm. Prisoners of war were sold off to the French and various other Europeans to be slaves in the New World. Many would end up in the slave markets of New Orleans, Charleston, Port-au-Prince

75

and parts unknown. Today it is a small town with an economy dependent on the dwindling tourist trade. Only 50 meters away is the river, an endless brown mirror that is as wide as it is flat. A junked passenger ferry sits useless in the water near the left bank. Domestic sounds, music and laundry hung to dry are evidence that this is someone's home. Docked at the bank are various brightly colored pinasses, with their thatched roofs and sturdy wood frames. The river men navigate the shallow muddy water with nothing but good balance and long bamboo poles. They carry people and goods from the opposite side into Segu for market days or other business. On market day everything is magnified. There is food, spices, animal hides, wood, salt, clothing, beads, cowrie shells, animals, household goods, and anything else that can be bought or sold, seemingly in bountiful abundance. People come from miles around by foot, donkey, car, motor scooter, or river. Many sellers come with their goods the night before and sleep on the levee at the riverbank until early the next morning. They will awaken and start selling as they do every market day.

Amadou Toure is a Songhai man from Gao, the ancient Songhai capital in the Sahara of northern Mali. He is tall and brown, with a friendly, respectful manner and a sharp goatee. As the head of the Tuareg artisans who have their various stalls neatly arranged on the hotel premises, he is a skillful salesman and a hard bargainer. He is 50 years old, but the years don't show on his face. He moves about Segu on a scooter, walks briskly and prays five times a day. He wraps his head and face in a long turban, sometimes showing only his eyes. If a customer gives him an unacceptable price, he covers his face as if to signify the end of negotiations. A sell will get the customer a warm smile. He doesn't smoke, and his drink of choice is green tea with mint. Helping him is his son and grandson. Being of two different mothers, the son is ten years old while the grandson is a young adult. Abdou, the son, has the air of a small, alert, and wise old man. His cleanly shaven head and bright clear eyes reinforce this. The Toures are a noble clan of the Songhai. Many of them own slaves and the men often take more than one wife. Amadou eagerly greets patrons his prospective customers. There is a group of U.S. embassy personnel on vacation, two African tourists from the diaspora and a Peace Corps volunteer walking by with her family who are visiting from the States. But first they must all wait until Amadou and the Tuareg craftsmen who work for him finish their prayers. The call to prayer punctuates each day, marking the time and giving order to daily life. They roll out their prayer mats on the sand and pray against a wall that is opposite Amadou's large tent filled with colorful, traditional merchandise. There is indigo cloth, bogolanfini, statues, decorative boxes and trunks, leather cushions, blankets, silver jewelry and artful trinkets too numerous to count. Everything is made with care and attention to detail. Amadou is interested to know about foreign lands and is familiar with many names and places in the U.S. When he is asked if he would ever like to go there, he says that he would like to see it, but only for a visit. He would return back home, he says. He loves his country and culture too much to leave it for long.

After a while, the conversation shifts to the subject of Ali Farka Toure, a distant relative. Amadou is proud, his eyes sparkle in the hot sun as he talks about the man's music and accomplishments. Ali Farka brought Songhai culture and music to the whole world. Matter of factly, Amadou mentions that Ali's griot lives in town. He asks if

I would like to meet him. I can't believe my good fortune. I envision an old ngoni player wise from years of singing the praises of the Toures while he advises them on the matters of nobility and household protocol. I cannot be more mistaken. My imagination did not prepare me for who I was about to meet. This would be the biggest surprise of all.

I WAS HIS SLAVE

"No one willingly chooses the yolk of slavery."
- Aeschylus

One day an older man in a beige colored boubou rides up on a blue moped. His head is clean shaven and he looks younger than his years. He is short and black as a thousand midnights. He moves about fluidly and sits on the sandy ground with ease, his legs folded underneath him. His eyes are bright and clear. By way of introduction, Amadou says that this man was Ali Farka Toure's griot, as others nod in agreement. His name is Hamdoun Kele. He and I agree to meet the next day at four o'clock in the afternoon. I ask Hamdoun about being Ali Farka Toure's griot. He quickly corrects me, letting me know that he was a slave to Ali's family. "J'etais son esclave"(I was his slave). I am surprised at how the words roll easily from his mouth. He says it proudly, with a smile. I wonder why Amadou told me that he was Ali's griot. The lines between the two occupations seem blurred, indicative of the low status often ascribed to griots. Both are virtually attached to their noble families for life. I think about my good fortune in running into Hamdoun here in Segu, hundreds of miles from Ali's hometown of Niafunke. I look around the sandy

79

streets and take in the scene. Donkeys, pedestrians and scooters slowly navigate the road nearby. Dust blows in from across the river, mixing in the warm, dry air with the faint smell of the timeless, muddy water. Small black flies flit about in the golden rays of the afternoon sun. The voices of nearby children at play mix with traditional music blasting from a radio in the distance. A donkey brays stubbornly as its owner beats his rump with a switch.

I recall my second visit to Niafunke in 2002 when I heard Ali Farka joking with his friend Bekaye Coulibaly, a Bambara man: "You are my slave!" There is a long history of Songhai versus Bambara, north versus south, Islam versus indigenous African religion. "We brought you Islam!" he exclaims, and everyone in the room laughs out loud. I can't believe my ears. This is like a Malian version of The Dozens, the game where the winner serves up the most artful, cutting insult imaginable. Who can imagine the same scenario in the US, where the children of slave masters can freely joke with and ridicule the children of slaves? It obviously means something very different to be a slave in Mali, then and now. Hamdoun explains how slavery works in Malian society. Blacks in the American slave system "could not eat with the master." He also says that the Africans brought to America were sold into slavery to be "thrown away." Captive Africans in the US were not valued as human beings in any way, shape or form. As it was once said in the Mississippi Delta, "Kill a nigger, hire another one. Kill a mule, buy another one." The plantation system viewed Black folk as expendable commodities, chattel to be used and discarded. Hamdoun clearly knows the difference between the brutal, murderous chattel slavery developed in the Americas and the slavery in Malian society bound by measures of tradition, honor and duty.

80

As he explains this difference, he looks back at Amadou who nods and smiles in agreement. "Over there [in the USA] you cannot eat with the nobles [master]." Here, in Mali it is commonplace. Of course in the US, even favored slaves who served whites in the 'Big House' had to eat their meals separately with separate dishes and utensils. Racism and white supremacy enforced the idea that Africans were somehow contaminated or unclean. Separation was enforced by law in every aspect of life. This white man's law relentlessly brutalized everything Black in order to keep the captive Africans in their proscribed places. Terrorist tactics such as cross-burnings, lynchings and beatings were the order of the day. There was no obligation on the part of the master and no protection was afforded the slave. They had no rights whatsoever.

Hamdoun explains that there is a code of conduct for the institution of bondage in Mali. If a slave needs money, his master gives it to him. Just this morning, Amadou had come to Hamdoun's house and gave his wife food and money. "Slavery here is not the same thing as you all experienced. With us here, every noble has their slave... your father took care of me, your child will take care of my child." This type of bondage is passed down through the generations so that every noble family is bound to a slave family. There are complex rules, verbal contracts and traditions which govern what is appropriate and what is not. "You, they took from here to take over there to throw you away, to mistreat you. Here, you cannot mistreat a slave. A person with a slave is obliged to feed them, to provide them with clothing. You must do everything for them." He explains that slaves are in charge of certain aspects of their masters' lives. For example, if a noble wants to marry a particular woman and the slave objects, then he cannot

81

take the woman as his wife. The noble is obligated to leave the woman. Hamdoun says, "It is me [with his wife] who cooks, who does everything." As such, it is the slave who dictates who can become the noble's wife since it is he who will have to do all the work for the woman. Though he has a low status, the slave has some measure of power in the household. "We are proud to do it!" says Hamdoun. He opens his arms wide for emphasis as his eyes flash with a serious intensity. There are obligations on both sides, for noble and slave. "Even if I do something stupid in town, I cannot be touched. They [the police] will come and tell you [the noble] something." Traditional slavery operates through contract, protocol and obligation. It is not freedom. But it has rules and customs which are uniform and cannot be violated. Captive Africans in the West were sold off just like livestock and they could be mistreated or killed for no reason. This is unthinkable in Mali. If he mistreats his slaves, a cruel master risks his good reputation in the community. "Because your father kept my father, you will keep me, and your child will keep my child." As Hamdoun speaks, I begin to realize that Amadou is his master.

Hamdoun talks while the warm afternoon sun flashes in his young/old man eyes. "It was me, Ali, Boni, Koita, Mangala. There were five of us. We played football together and we played music together. Me, I played like this." Amadou mimes playing the njarka, a one-string violin. "Boni played pitiga [thumb piano], Ali played a one-string, I played the njarka. We were in the market, and all the time, every night, there were people surrounding us as we played our music. Mangala would bring a guitar. It was there that Ali began to play the guitar...three of us played and one sang. At this time, Mangala had the guitar and now Ali left the one string and began playing the guitar." It is 1960, the year of Mali's independence from France. The five friends are close in age, all in their late teens or early twenties. Ali begins to play Mangala's guitar more and more often. This irritates Mangala, who now refuses to let Ali touch his guitar. Everyone is saying, "It is Ali who knows how to play. You should give it to Ali!" Mangala does not like this at all. Before too long he takes his guitar back. In fact, the guitar belongs to Mangala's brother Mamadou. He is a driver for a local government official, which pays him enough money to afford simple luxuries such as an acoustic guitar. Ali does not let Mangala's refusal to let him play the guitar stop him. He begins to work and save money to buy his own guitar.

It is through farming, his other love in life after music, that he is able to earn the money he needs to buy his own instrument. He thinks about music constantly while he is working the land. If he is not farming, he can be found playing music in the market, no matter the time of day. He is first and foremost a man of the soil, a son of the desert. This is what makes his music so powerful. Farming is in his blood. He traverses the planet playing his music, but he will always go back to farming. And whenever he is farming, he is always listening to music. There is a living connection between the sound and the soil, the sonic and the organic. Just like his old blues brothers from the Black belt of the American south, he knows the soil and grew up working in it. He loves the different languages of the vast nation - Bambara, Pulaar, Tomasheck, Bozo - and he pays tribute to them by learning their songs. He loves not only his remote hometown of Niafunke; he loves the whole of Mali, from the dirt on up.

They all play football together and Ali Farka drives them around. Their dilapidated old Renault has no brakes, and they all have to push it to get it started. When they reach their destination they all climb on top to bring their instruments down. Hamdoun explains that once they went to the Niafunke airport for a gig. One of them puts rocks in front of the old car and that is how they stop it. They play, and when they finish they start all over again in the next place. This is how Ali's music career begins, playing in local villages near his home in Niafunke, much like the djeli do. Even though he is doing what he loves, he is not a djeli. No one understands why a noble would be so drawn to a life in music. It is forbidden. His father has passed away and his uncle is strict and unforgiving. He doesn't understand his nephew who takes every opportunity he has to play music with is friends. Oumar Toure says that his uncle was the only man whom Ali was ever afraid of. The elder Toure beats him severely to keep him in line. This older generation dismisses the ambitions of their children when they do not conform to tradition. Parents know well that life is hard, and many are hard on their children in return. This is not because they want to be mean to their children, but so that the child will be able to go into the world and not be swallowed up by its harsh realities. As many old folks used to say, "Spare the rod and spoil the child." Years later, when his uncle is on his deathbed, he apologizes to Ali for being so harsh. He says he just wanted to make Ali a man.

Even today, Mali is a society bound by tradition. This was all the more true during Ali's youth prior to the end of colonization. Like any Malian youth, Ali's family expect him to follow in the footsteps of his parents. Everyone, every caste has its place. You do as your parents did before you with no exceptions. But in this new era of independence, young Ali Farka Toure is defying more than a thousand years of tradition by simply playing music. He plays in the market with his small group of friends, hiding his ngoni in the market every night so that his family won't find out what he is doing when he is not farming. Music is a secret pleasure. As Hamdoun Kele recalls, "When he wanted to play, everyone said he was crazy. They did everything to make him leave music, but they couldn't do it. He loved music so much. Once he heard music, that was it for him. He loved music very much." Ali's routine with his friends is to play music in the market all day until midnight or one o'clock in the morning. Then they go to the cinema. After the cinema they go back to play music before finally going to sleep.

In 1968, a few years after he first meets his lifelong confidante and percussionist Oumar Toure, Ali begins working at Radio Mali in Bamako. The bustling, teeming capitol city is worlds away from the vast stillness of northern Mali. Hamdoun explains that "Everything that people would show Ali how to do, he would pick it up easily. Once you show him how to do it one time, he will quickly learn how to do it with no problem." Ali works for several years with Radio Mali, where he first meets Cheick Tidiane Seck, the famed keyboardist and multi-instrumentalist. Short in stature and big in spirit, Cheick Tidiane is a Bambara man from Segu who will make his name playing keyboard with the Super Rail Band and later with Salif Keita ("The Golden Voice of Africa") and Les Ambassadeurs. Cheick Tidiane's resume will later include projects with such jazz luminaries as Hank Jones, Dee Dee Bridgewater and Joe Zawinul.

The two will remain friends for the rest of Ali's life. Ali records several albums while at Radio Mali, exposing many more people in Mali and elsewhere to his profound musical talents. His tenure at Radio Mali eventually comes to an end. According to Hamdoun, they do everything to make him stay there. "But he said no, he wanted to keep moving, because the people criticized him there because he was so good. They didn't like him, so he quit." Ali returns to music full-time and he earns more recognition and fame as the years go by.

By now, Ali is respected as not only a great musician, but as a man of the people. Looking back, Hamdoun remembers that, "Everybody loved him. But after some time the people began to be jealous of him. But he loved everybody, women, children, old people. Even in Niafunke there were people who did not like Ali. There were those who were against him. He became the mayor, and many people were not happy with this. But he donated seven million CFA to the mayor's office. He paid everything. He increased the amount of money in the treasury by seven million CFA ($14,000.00 US), but there were people who really did not like it. Even now if you ask around Niafunke, there are people who would say that Niafunke killed him. Even now, there are people saying this. Have you seen his house? Everybody went there to eat, at the house. But when they would leave, they would talk about him. But Ali gave to everyone because he had the means." Oumar Toure later recalls that whenever anyone had a need or a proposal for a business Ali Farka readily provided the necessary funds. He buys generators for the entire town of Niafunke so that everyone would have access to electricity. Ali does not play music simply to entertain. Music is a means to an end. It is a way to develop his community and

86

educate others about culture, morality, history and tradition. Being a successful farmer and businessman, he does not rely solely upon his musical career to provide for his family. Perhaps this explains why he is able to stop touring later in life and become mayor of Niafunke. He is fully devoted to his culture and his community. His music is an expression of this devotion. Ali also invests his own money in a cassette and record-pressing operation which sells Malian music throughout the entire country, thus providing a livelihood for scores of young music vendors who sell in the streets of Bamako and across Mali. This business, along with his transport, garage, hotels, cattle and land is the economic backbone in this town of mud-brick and French colonial buildings on the river. Yet for all his eventual success this is still the same man who declares with a smile that "poverty and humility is the way." He displays no obvious material wealth, no flashy cars, no nice watches, no European fashion, no fine champagne. He is the earth, uncomplicated, direct, organic and raw. This man knows who he is and his place in the world. He sings in languages that few outside of his region of West Africa understand, yet despite this the whole world is under the spell of his desert blues.

Later in life, Hamdoun Kele sees his master less frequently, as continuous touring keeps Ali away from Mali for months at a time. The last time he sees Ali Farka alive is here in Segu. He is staying at the Hotel Joliba and calls Hamdoun to check on him and give him some money. Ali Farka loves to drive the open desert, even though banditry is common. "You know even when he left here with his vehicle to go to Niafunke, there were people who tried to trap him on the road. Two, three times they attacked him on the road. He had a good car. If you tried to catch him you could not do it. In Niafunke, if he parked his car he would take off the tires. If not, people would come and steal them. The next day, if he wanted to leave, he would put them back on again. There were always people trying to do him bad. People were nasty, they didn't care." Just like the crabs who fight each other in the barrel, those who do not like Ali do their best to try to bring him down. Success brings the good and the bad, enmity and friendship, and everything in between. When Ali finally passed away, Hamdoun remembers that "everyone was saying how good he was. There was nothing bad that you could say about him. You could not say that he did anything bad to anyone. You could only say that he did his best."

Hamdoun says a prayer for Ali Farka. He spreads his hands open, palms out and bows his head which shines like the blackest obsidian. We are all sitting in the sand, listening to Ali Farka's music. Hamdoun makes a solemn prayer in Arabic, opens his eyes for a few seconds, then closes them as his hands wash down his face in a gesture of cleansing. As he speaks his benediction ancient notes slither out from Ali's guitar. We feel the snap and clap of the calabash, the beat of the congas, the wail of the njarka and the chanting of the background singers. The sound is precise and nimble, at once both fresh and ancient. We all know it's a recording, but at this moment Ali Farka has come back to life. He was only sleeping. The prayer finishes and the air is heavy with the sound and soul of a great man. Dusk approaches and the various vendors begin to pack up their wares. Hamdoun looks exhausted, shaken. Ali is in the air, his spirit among us. Afterwards, we have some 'gunpowder' green tea, strong and sugary with plenty of fresh mint. Hamdoun talks about Vieux (Boureima) Farka Toure. Vieux has taken up where his father left off, bringing the real Songhai desert blues guitar to an ever widening audience. Hamdoun says that he is just like Ali. "He has such a good heart." He says this with love and admiration in his voice. There is a genuine warmth. This is a man who is presented by others as a griot, but who is quick to correct the misinformed, proudly declaring that he was Ali Farka's slave. As the descendant of those who were stolen away from Africa and enslaved by Europeans, I cannot at all imagine their being proud of their situation. I am reminded by this elder that the slavery my ancestors endured in the New World and slavery as it exists in Mali are two entirely different things. But who can say that this humble man sitting across from me in the sand here in Segu never dreamt of freedom, that he never longed for independence? I am left to wonder.

LEGACY

"In aiding the young, we demonstrate our hope and faith in the future."
- H.I.M. Haile Selassie I

$\mathcal{A}$li Farka Toure made an impression everywhere he went, whether he was at home in Mali or traveling the world. His mastery of the guitar was unsurpassed. He drew people in with his warmth, his sincerity, and the respect that he accorded to everyone he came in contact with. His love of laughter was balanced by a noble, dignified composure. Despite his high status, he treated everyone equally. He was genuine, unique and one hundred percent human. He was unforgettable. Samba Toure says it best: "Ali Farka is a man that...if one says they are talking about him, it could take hours and one would not finish." He was a man who was proud of his origins, his culture, and his nation. Though he had the means and the international recognition to travel far and wide, he always returned home to Mali, to the roots. There have been many Africans who have stayed in Europe or America for years, preferring the spoils and comforts of Western life to the sometimes difficult existence they have encountered at home. This was clearly not the case with Ali, who quit touring so that he

91

could devote more of his time to his family and the development of his community. There is no simple way to sum up the life of such an influential and well-loved figure. But we can give the reader an idea of who this great man was through the words of some of those who knew him best.

Cheick Tidiane Seck has known Ali Farka since early the seventies, when they were both active in the Bamako music scene. When Cheick was a member of the Rail Band, Ali Farka himself recorded many of their concerts at the Buffet de la Gare, a Bamako restaurant and legendary hotspot. Cheick recalled his old friend with a deep admiration that has stood the test of time. "The humor of Ali was so great. We grew up together. He's a big brother, but we share musically. He was humble, you know. Every time we met, he would call me 'master'. I would say, 'No Ali, I'm not.' Ali was very talented, you know." At this stage of his career Ali had adapted a version of the James Brown songs, "Man's World' and 'There Was a Time' to his native Songhai. He also sang John Lee Hooker's 'Mean, Mean Woman' in his native tongue. These songs, along with his own compositions and his versions of traditional repertoire, helped to spread the word about the masterful musician from Niafunke.

Ali's music made a lasting impression on Cheick: "The way he played the music, he had his own language. Ali, he had his own touch, mixed with his influence taken from the African-American blues. He had his own way of playing coming from the north of Mali. I know this kind of pentatonic scale is different. It's a different language. They [musicians from the north] have a kind of oriental vibe." Legendary giants of Malian music such as the singer and ngoni player Banzoumana "The Lion" Cissoko, Djelibaba, and Siramory Diabate, the great djelimousso (female djeli) had a profound influence on Ali's music. Ali played with many of the great elder ngoni players of his time. In fact the way he played the guitar transformed the sound of this tempered western instrument into that of the ngoni. His playing transcended the instrument. This was a noble man, one forbidden by tradition to play music, but who forged his path by learning the music of the great djelis who were his elders. "He was somebody so humble, that when he played, it was from the heart. He touches you. That is not school who give that, you know. If you conform to what you are playing, you touch the energy, the global energy." Cheick's last memory of Ali was in Paris at his hotel near the Place d'Italie. This was in 2006 and Ali was very sick. During his visit with Ali, they talked and reminisced about the past and all of their shared experiences in music. Though he was already very ill, Ali played a concert in Paris. "It was the last show we did together in Paris. Ousman Kouyate, Toumani Diabate, Jean Phillipe Rykiel and myself. We played with him. He was sitting on a chair because he could not stand up." Ali made his biggest mark in the world with his music, but Cheick talks about the man. When asked about Ali's legacy, he has three simple words: "humility, generosity and love." Such was the measure of the man.

Younger players such as Samba Toure and Bassekou Kouyate can bear witness to Ali's kindness. When Samba first came to Bamako from Timbuktu, he fronted a band called Farafina Delo (Africa Star) that specialized in Congolese soukous music. Soukous is a hot, high-energy, extremely danceable music that is popular throughout Africa. This is what many Bamako audiences would listen to when drinking and dancing the nights away. This is in contrast

93

to the droning and chanting that characterizes the traditional music of the northern deserts – what many in Mali
refer to as the blues. When Ali heard Samba's music he
advised him, "My son you are really talented but it would
be better to do the music of your home." Like Ali, Samba is
also Songhai. Samba replied, "Ton-ton (uncle) our northern music is slow in comparison to here in Bamako." Ali
was a steadfast advocate for the traditional Songhai music,
even though for many years he struggled to make a living
playing this music. In the beginning, he didn't earn more
than the price of cigarettes, but he remained committed to
his music and culture. Samba recalls, "Ali told me that I
must do this music, the blues of our homeland. Where we
come from, we know the blues like the uniform that the
doctor wears when he goes to the hospital!" This music is
everywhere. Soon Samba begins to take lessons from him.
This led to Samba becoming a member of Ali's group and
touring Europe and North America beginning in 1999 and
2000.

Ali also encouraged Samba to develop his own career, telling Samba, "It is time to make your new album."
Ali produced and financed the record for his young protégé.
Samba titled his debut release 'Songhai Blues.' Samba
learned one lesson from Ali that he would never forget.
"One day I was playing, because often he would bring out
two guitars and we would do our thing. When I was playing I was looking at the guitar neck and he told me, 'No.
You need to play with the spirit.' Because he told me that
the blind man who plays does not see the guitar neck. It is
the spirit. He told me that when you play with the spirit, if
it is up here [in the head] it will come out here [the fingers].
Every time I play I think of this advice and I think of him.
Really, from the time I touch the guitar, I am only thinking

about Ali Farka." Ali gave Samba a sound system and a quality guitar befitting a professional player. "He told me, 'Son, go and choose the guitar that you want.' Samba 's gratitude for Ali's efforts to help him have only grown stronger with the passage of time. "Since Farka passed away until today, thirty minutes have not passed without thinking about him. I only listen to his music."

Bassekou Kouyate tells a similar story about his time with the Master. "Ali would call me all the time, telling me, 'You have a hand like a black diamond. You have to do something so that the world will know you now. They need to know that you are here. What are you waiting for?" Ali was always pushing the younger players, encouraging them to develop their careers instead of just being content to play with Ali. "Why don't you do something for yourself?" Ali found a producer for his debut album, which Bassekou titled 'Segu' after the region along the Niger that is his birthplace. It is not common for elder musicians such as Ali to spend so much time and effort helping those who will come behind them. But Ali Farka was not common. It is noteworthy that when Bassekou talks about his first impression of Ali, he does not even mention the music. He loved his music very much, but he speaks most passionately about the quality of the man, his character. He strived to help the younger musicians such as Bassekou, Afel Bocoum, Toumani Diabate, Oumou Sangare and many others. He was selfless in his promotion of the next generation of musicians.

We have seen that since his youth in Niafunke, Ali had been exposed to the ngoni through the djeli who played for his father. As a young man he played with all of the greatest Malian ngoni players -- legends of their in-

95

strument such as Djelibaba, Tidiane, and Laoka -- whose names are highly respected by musicians and non-musicians alike. It is no surprise that when asked about the legacy that Ali Farka Toure left, Bassekou speaks of the ngoni. "That is how Ali was able to give the sound of the ngoni on his guitar. Because it is not the sound of the guitar...it is the sound of the ngoni interpreted on his guitar." When western music journalists described Ali Farka as the bluesman from Mali who learned to play listening to John Lee Hooker records, they are displaying their ignorance of this important fact. His reference was not the guitar, or even the blues as westerners would know it, but the ngoni, which has its roots in the ancient cultures of the Nile Valley, long before the formation of the Mali empire. This is why he would often say that blues was a color. The blues influenced his music, but he would assert matter-of-factly that "my music is older than the blues." He may have been illiterate in European languages but Ali Farka Toure was well aware of the history behind the music that he played. Perhaps if he had become famous playing the ngoni or the njarka (one string violin) instead of the guitar, he may never have been known as the Malian bluesman, since the guitar is so closely identified with the blues. He was a true lover of blues music and understood more than most the musical kinship between his Songhai culture and that of the blues. One cannot say the word 'blues' in Mali today without mentioning his name.

Bassekou gives Ali much of the credit for popularizing the ngoni. Savane, the album that was released shortly after his death in 2006 featured Bassekou's masterful playing on the instrument. "The people would say, 'Ah what is that? That's the ngoni?" Many people around the world learned about the ngoni through this album." Bassekou's participation in the recording came about quickly and without much fanfare. Ali had mentioned to him before that he wanted him to play on his next record. One day he was driving in his car on the way home and his cellphone rang. It was the Englishman Nick Gold. He asked him to come the next morning to Studio Bogolan, a recording studio in Bamako where countless Mali music classics have been produced. "Ali needs you. He wants to try something with you." Bassekou arrived the next morning at ten o'clock and as soon as he walked in the door he found Ali dancing, fully animated. Upon seeing the young ngoni fola (ngoni player), he got even more excited. "Hey Bassekou! Viens ici!" ("Come here!") Ali was happy to see his young friend. He told Bassekou to sit down while he excitedly shouted for Yves, the French sound engineer, to come and set up the microphones to record the session. He took out his guitar and began to play the piece, 'Savane.' After only two minutes of practice, Ali shouted for the microphone. "Ok I'm ready. Let's go!" 'Savane' would be Ali's last record as a solo artist (his final recording, with Toumani Diabate, In the Heart of the Moon, was also released posthumously).

With this masterpiece, Ali and company captured the raw, sublime sound of the Songhai music for which he became famous. As always, the sound of the ngoni was a crucial part of the production. The union of sound between that instrument and the guitar set the whole vibe. Speaking about the session years later, Bassekou sounds almost incredulous. "Two minutes of practice, two minutes! So that was the album Savane. He left me a lot of space so that I could play well, so that people [who were listening] could say, 'Ah! What is that?'" The year after Ali's passing, Bassekou released his first record, Segu Blue, which featured his tribute to Ali, 'Lament for Ali Farka.' Talk-

97

ing about the passing of the noble from Niafunke, the tone of Bassekou's voice shifts from happiness to a quiet reverence. "I traveled a lot with him. We did a lot of concerts and we were always together. The last concert we played in France...we came back to Bamako. We were supposed to go back to Europe, but Ali was sick and he could not do it. That is how the project ended. Me, I continued with my group and Toumani continued with his group."

"Ali had a good heart. It is very rare to see a great musician, a great singer who lays back behind the scenes and encourages the younger players." It seems that everyone who speaks about Ali Farka has a story to tell about how he helped them. Ali would often tell Bassekou and Toumani that it was their turn now, that his turn was finished. "The world should know that you are there. You and Toumani, now it's your turn. Me, I am finished, I have had my career. It's your turn now." Though he was already world famous, Ali was content to sit back and push the younger ones forward. Though many did not know the severity of the cancer that Ali was fighting, it is clear that he knew he did not have long to live. He supported the younger generation of musicians until the very end. His generosity did not limit itself to his fellow Malians. He was glad to teach anyone who expressed a genuine interest and respect for his music and culture. There were times when Ali received strangers into his home who had traveled two or three days by pinasse and over bumpy dirt roads just to come and sit at the feet of a legend. It didn't matter to him that he didn't know them. Everyone was warmly received. He knew that Niafunke is not an easy place to get to. He respected the fact that people cared enough to put in the extra effort to reach his small outpost in the Sahara.

I remember one hot and dusty evening in Niafunke in 2001 playing with Ali. Insects swarmed around the fluorescent light on the wall of Ali's house at the edge of the river. Lizards perched on the wall nearby, waiting for their next meal. Even though I was unfamiliar with the droning sound of Songhai guitar and the traditional rhythms of the north, he took time to show me the basics of his style. I remember him telling me with a smile that I have a lot to learn about his guitar style. He was right. I was learning a new musical language. When we played the blues together it was effortless. But the other music that he played needed to be studied and learned. There is a difference between these two styles, even though they both belong to the same tree. The blues is the fruit and Africa is the root. It is the source. So he could easily meet a blues player at his level without having to change his playing or approach to the music. His music was everything that we Black folk had forgotten about the music of our ancestors. At the end of one of our evening sessions recording in the small house on the river in Niafunke, I was struggling to learn a passage I had just heard him play and he simply looked at me and said, "Tu le merites!" ("You are worth it!") Ali Farka Toure did his best to help every musician that he worked with, no matter where they came from. His music was great, but the man was even greater.

The last time I've seen Ali Farka Toure alive was in December, 2004. I am in southern France with my seven year-old son. We have come to Privas, a small medieval village about an hour's drive outside of Lyon. The homes here are built among large rock formations and resemble caves. They are virtually indistinguishable from the environment. The landscape is typically mediterrannean -- arid, rocky and covered in small trees and scrub brush. It is dark outside and freezing cold. We are guests at the home of a French man and his Senegalese wife who are Ali's hosts for the afternoon. It is a small gathering, but the anticipation of the imminent arrival of the noble farmer from Niafunke makes it feel like a big event. We wait for nearly an hour and then suddenly Ali appears in the small doorway, voice booming as he greets the small group. He stoops down to enter the room and it is instantly filled with his wide smile and booming voice. Warmth fills the room like a desert sunrise. Accompanying him are Nick Gold from World Circuit records and a friend of Ali's from northern Mali. After more greetings are exchanged and introductions are offered around the small room, Ali and I walk outside to talk.

He tells me about his latest bout with cancer, saying with a smile, "Sur le point de mourrir...dead!" ("I was almost dead!") He is happy, fearless. This warrior has won this battle and he is ready to go back into the fray. He is much thinner and the skin on his face is noticeably tighter, though his complexion is still Black albeit a little grey at the edges. These are his battle scars. But his spirit hasn't dimmed. He still has the same smiling eyes and easy laughter. We come out of the cold and sit around a table in the warmth of the dining room as a documentary film crew records our exchange. A fire glows in the fireplace. The king is here. He treats everyone as his equal, as his friend. Respect, nobility, dignity come naturally to this man. He comes from a place where these qualities are still valued and celebrated. He explains that he has recently been elected mayor of Niafunke. He has a lot of

-- expanding electrical servic‹
He has always been concerne‹
always working towards a better to-
‹l population. Now that he has retired
‹ is in the twilight of his life, he is devoting
‹aining energies to Niafunke. The previous
‹ayed a concert to raise funds for a new development project. At the end of his life, he is wealthy and successful, but he remains focused on helping others. He says
that there is so much to do. As the proverb says, 'to whom
much is given, much is expected.' I ask him about Doudou,
his youngest son whom I met the last time I visited him
in Niafunke. He smiles and produces a picture of the boy,
now a toddler. He hands it to me and I look at it for a moment. When I go to hand it back he tells me that the photo
is mine to keep. It was a simple gesture, but this small gift
meant a lot to me. Little did I know that this would be our
last meeting. Within 18 months he will be gone.

He doesn't leave without endearing himself to my
son Isaac. At first the boy is shy and reserved, but after
five minutes with Ali Farka they are playing and laughing
like old friends. Ali tells me that the next time we travel
we must come visit him in Niafunke. He looks at Isaac
and says, "Leave him with me...I'll take him there." I can
tell he means what he says. It is getting late and Ali must
prepare for the upcoming trip to Paris to see his doctor. We
say our goodbyes and he walks out the door, gets in a car
and is driven away. We watch the car's tail lights as they
disappear into the winter darkness. Although I came to
France to play a concert I now understand the real reason I
came here. I give thanks for this final visit with the desert
lion, Ali Farka Toure.

Discography

1976 - Ali Touré Farka (Sonafric 50016-LP)

1976 - Spécial « Biennale du Mali » (Sonafric 50020-LP)

1978 - Biennale (Sonafric 50032-LP)

1979 - Ali Touré Farka (Sonafric 50060-LP)

1980 - Ali Touré dit Farka (Sonafric 50085-LP)

1984 - Ali Farka Touré (Red) (Sonodisc/Esperance 5558)

1988 - Ali Farka Touré (Green) (Sonodisc/Esperance 8448)

1988 - Ali Farka Touré (World Circuit WCD007 / Mango 9826)

1990 - African Blues (Shanachie 65002) (originally released as Ali Farka Touré (Green))

1990 - The River (World Circuit WCD017 / Mango 9897)

1992 - The Source (World Circuit WCD030 / Hannibal 1375) with Taj Mahal

1994 - Talking Timbuktu (World Circuit WCD040 / Hannibal 1381) (with Ry Cooder)

1996 - Radio Mali (World Circuit WCD044 / Nonesuch 79569) (remastered selections of original albums from 1975 through 1980)

1999 - Niafunké (World Circuit WCD054 / Hannibal 1443)
2002 - Mississippi to Mali (Rounder B0000DJZA1)(with Corey Harris)

2004 - Red&Green (World Circuit WCD070 / Nonesuch 79882) (remastered original albums from 1984 and 1988)
2005 - In the Heart of the Moon (World Circuit WCD072 / Nonesuch 79920) (with Toumani Diabaté
and Ry Cooder)

2006 - Savane (World Circuit WCD075 / Nonesuch 79965)

2010 - Ali and Toumani - (World Circuit/Nonesuch Records) with Toumani Diabaté

Source: Wikipedia

Credits from The Author

Thank you:

Haile Selassie I, the Ancestors and all my relations, Fannie Fiddmont, Lisa Leigh, Gerri Malone, Jennifer Watt, Yared Getachew, Benita Johnson, George Rezendes, Tomomi Hoshina, Jan Trasen, Ward Whitehorn, Anne McCarty, Joel Schwartz, Vera Hoar, Angel Arnaudas, Laura Mello, Sylvie Degabriel, Seydou Ndiaye, Carson, Scott Peek, Ken Dorfman, Valerie Turner, Happy Traum, Julian Atkinson, Craig and Stephanie Smith, Perter Carey, Dan Bowden, Roz Powell, Josh Gershtenson, Francis Hemming, Michael Ng, Ron Weinstock, Khaliq and Naima Wares-Akers, Siriporn Umpherston, Wamuhu Waweru, Stanley Taylor, and Jeanne Quigley and Ife Robinson.

Edited by Khaliq Akers.

Book cover artwork by Corey "Rashid" Williams-El

For my children Isaac, Jazz and Mansa